Touching
THE HEM

a biblical response
to physical suffering

Elizabeth A. Johnson

AMBASSADOR INTERNATIONAL
GREENVILLE, SOUTH CAROLINA & BELFAST, NORTHERN IRELAND

www.ambassador-international.com

TOUCHING THE HEM
A Biblical Response to Physical Suffering

Printed in the United States of America

ISBN: 978-1-62020-205-0
eISBN: 978-1-62020-303-3

All Scripture quotations, unless otherwise indicated, are taken from the King James Version.

Cover design & typesetting: Matthew Mulder
E-book conversion: Anna Riebe

AMBASSADOR INTERNATIONAL
Emerald House
427 Wade Hampton Blvd.
Greenville, SC 29609, USA
www.ambassador-international.com

AMBASSADOR BOOKS
The Mount
2 Woodstock Link
Belfast, BT6 8DD, Northern Ireland, UK
www.ambassadormedia.co.uk

The colophon is a trademark of Ambassador

For Barbara Hanson,
who is now touching the hem of Christ's eternal garment.

Table of Contents

PART V

A Look at God's Response

Preface

WHAT IS A CHRISTIAN TO do when faced with sickness? This is a question which I have struggled to answer for several years now, as I deal with a serious life-long illness. Although it may go into remission, it could return at any time.

My chronic illness means years of multiple medications and respective side effects. It means being somewhat housebound due to a low immune system and inconsistent energy levels. It has led to chronic fatigue, monthly doctor visits and lab tests, occasional emergency surgeries, and a new way of life. It means a new normal for me and those closest to me.

Before my diagnosis, I considered God's healing power as something reserved for someone else. I knew, of course, about the healings in the New Testament. I had heard stories of intercessors and those prayed for receiving miraculous healing. I knew God was *able* to heal, but I had never really personalized that truth. Then I ended up in the hospital, close to death, and suddenly the question of healing became extremely personal.

Once I was coherent enough to think, my initial response was tremendous gratitude for still being alive. I had not known how serious my condition was when I had been admitted to the hospital. When I found out, I wept tears of joy at being given another chance at life, no matter how difficult it was expected to be.

Then, as my enthusiasm began to wane, I settled into a new routine. A new sense of normal started to evolve. I grew accustomed to having the illness, being tired, and facing difficulties unfamiliar and inconceivable to my peers. I still did not seriously consider the possibility of being healed. I was dutifully taking my medications, seeing my doctors, and hoping my illness might eventually improve.

I slowly began to notice people talking about healing: Does God heal? Whom does God heal? Why does God *not* heal? I began to resent the little by-the-ways preachers insert into their sermons. I felt their monologues on healing did not apply to me.

My sickness was not due to sin, nor could it have been avoided by anything such as personal habits or lifestyle changes. I was not living in sin; I was faithful in my prayer life and church attendance; and I was trying to live for God's continued glory. Yet, I was not being healed. I felt my case had been overlooked somehow. I began to struggle with discouragement and even resentment whenever someone talked about God's power to heal.

Then something changed my attitude, and I can only attribute it to the Holy Spirit's gentle nudging. I began to pray earnestly for healing. I went to the Scriptures, searching for passages regarding sickness and healing. I sought examples of those who had been healed as a result of prayer and those who remained sick. I searched for materials about the topic and found a great dearth.

Many charismatics have written books and articles about healing, asserting their dramatic views of faith healings. Others have written from the mind-over-matter viewpoint, proclaiming if we would believe ourselves to be healed, or have enough faith, then we would find ourselves healed. Still others have purported, if we were truly living in God's will, then we would not even be dealing with sickness. None of these views, however, seem to agree with Scripture—the standard of truth by which everything must be measured.

There are, of course, many books outlining generalized topics regarding trouble and suffering that stay true to Scripture. There are innumerable studies on the character and works of God, which refer to and expound upon what is already established in the Word of God. There is a myriad of resources available regarding our response to these things. Yet, where is a resource about healing that is biblically accurate, or even better, a resource that combines all these things and remains true to God's Word?

This is what I have endeavored to do through this study. It is not only for my personal enrichment, but also with the prayer that it may help others who face the trial of a long-term physical suffering.

Acknowledgements

I BELIEVE AN AUTHOR'S WHOLE life enters into his work, including those the author has known, worked with, fellowshipped with, and sat under. I would be remiss if I did not mention some of those people and their contributions to this book.

First and foremost, my blessed Redeemer has given me grace through this great trial of illness, granted me His divine strength, and taught me about His perfect peace and abundant joy. He has graciously turned my illness into an opportunity to minister; He has given me the talent to write, time to study, and opportunities to put this book together. Unto Him be all the glory!

My beloved husband has been with me through the darkest hours of my illness and the subsequent ups–and–downs, yet he has never once wavered in his love and care for me. He has spent countless hours answering questions, giving suggestions, and encouraging and supporting me in every way. He is truly a picture of Christ's love, and worthy of all my love and respect.

My parents have supported and cheered me on since the beginning of this project. They have helped in so many ways, with more time and love than I could ever hope to repay. Could ever a daughter ask for better parents?

My childhood pastor, Dr. Robert Hanson, taught me from the

beginning to search the Scriptures as the Bereans. His preaching instilled in me a love for studying God's Word and a desire to seek His truth, which has certainly shaped my life's direction.

Other dear friends and family have been so encouraging throughout this project, offering countless prayers for physical strength and mental acuity, as well as more tangible forms of support. There are many names I could mention, but I particularly want to thank my grandparents, Mom and Dad J., Catherine V., Sarah B., Heidi H., Pastor and Elaine, and my families at Bible Baptist Church and Faith Baptist Church.

Introduction

And a certain woman, which had an issue of blood twelve years,
And had suffered many things of many physicians, and had spent all
that she had, and was nothing bettered, but rather grew worse, When
she had heard of Jesus, came in the press behind, and touched his gar-
ment. For she said, If I may touch but his clothes, I shall be whole.
And straightway the fountain of her blood was dried up; and she felt in
her body that she was healed of that plague.

And Jesus, immediately knowing in himself that virtue had gone
out of him, turned him about in the press, and said, Who touched
my clothes? And his disciples said unto him, Thou seest the multitude
thronging thee, and sayest thou, Who touched me? And he looked
round about to see her that had done this thing. But the woman fear-
ing and trembling, knowing what was done in her, came and fell down
before him, and told him all the truth. And he said unto her, Daughter,
thy faith hath made thee whole; go in peace, and be whole of thy plague.

—Mark 5:25–34

IF ANY WOMAN EVER FOUND herself in a seemingly hopeless
situation, this was the woman. For twelve long years she had suffered in many areas of her life. She dealt with physical pain, fatigue,
and frustration as she visited doctor after doctor in search of a cure.

Even after all those medical visits, after all their attempts to help her, she was "nothing bettered, but rather grew worse." How frustrating this situation must have been for her!

She also faced financial hardship—this account says she "had spent all that she had." Consider emptying your pockets, bank accounts, savings accounts—whatever resources you may have—in search of something so elusive. She might as well have just thrown all her money to the poor so someone could have visibly benefited from it!

Scripture does not say whether she went into debt, but it is likely. If she was searching that hard and long for a cure, she may have been indebted to some of the physicians for years after she finally was healed.

Also, she would have faced social challenges. According to Old Testament laws, which most Jewish people of that time still practiced faithfully, anyone with any issues of blood would have been considered unclean:

> *And if a woman have an issue of her blood many days out of the time of her separation, or if it run beyond the time of her separation; all the days of the issue of her uncleanness shall be as the days of her separation: she shall be unclean* (Leviticus 15:25).

She would have been considered a social outcast; no man would have desired her, no women would have wanted fellowship with her, no one would have attempted to be with her in any way. For it would have meant they, too, would then be considered unclean.

Truly, this woman's situation could have been considered hopeless. Yet, when she heard Jesus would be passing through her area, she stepped out in faith to meet Him. She ignored the social awkwardness and physical discomfort, and reached out with confidence. He was the great Healer she had heard about, and she simply had not given up hope she might be healed! ✗

Her faith, and the actions of her faith, brought the result she had been so earnestly seeking for twelve years. As soon as she touched the hem of Jesus' garment, "straightway the fountain of her blood was dried up; and she felt in her body that she was healed of that plague."

Not only was she immediately aware of her healing, but Christ Himself also turned around and brought the crowd's attention to her, announcing her faith and subsequent healing to all who listened. She was made an example to the crowd that day, and to the world throughout the rest of time through Scripture, simply because she exercised her faith to go and touch His hem.

So, the questions for us as we think about this woman's story are: Does God still heal in modern times as He did back then? Can believers today still experience the same divine power of being restored to physical wholeness? In order to answer these questions accurately, many things must be considered.

First, we must look at who our God claims to be. Does He claim to know our situation entirely? More specifically, does He claim to know our individual circumstances and needs? Does He still have the power to heal, if He desires to do so? Second, we must consider all the works God has done throughout history. In reviewing His past works, we can anticipate how He may work in the present and future.

Once we confirm who our God is and what He has done for us, we can look at our circumstances. Why do we even have to deal with sickness? What is its purpose in our lives? Does sickness serve the same purpose in everyone? In order to answer these questions, we must consider examples from the Old and New Testaments, as well as cases from modern times. Enough of God's people throughout history have dealt with sickness to provide some reasons and purposes for illness within our lives.

Finally, after considering God and our circumstances, we must then consider our response. How do we reconcile the loving-kindness of God and the difficulties of sickness? Should we trust Him to remove the sickness? Do we attempt to use physical means to find healing? Can we even hope for healing? If we hope for healing, what if its manifestation does not come immediately? What is our responsibility while we are waiting for healing?

These are questions with varying answers, depending upon interpretation. This is when theories abound—some biblically accurate, some not. There are many in the world today who would try to sell their own answers for these questions, derived from human philosophy and earthly wisdom.

However, we are told in 1 John 4:1 to "believe not every spirit, but try the spirits whether they are of God: because many false prophets are gone out into the world." We must follow the example of the Bereans, who "received the word with all readiness of mind, and searched the scriptures daily, whether those things were so" (Acts 17:11).

So we must weigh everything against the standard of Scripture, not merely accepting every message the world gives us, but studying and meditating personally upon the Word of God. Being discerning believers, we must search for the answers to life's hard questions in the very same Word of God, which provides all we need for life and godliness:

All scripture is given by inspiration of God, and is profitable for doctrine, for reproof, for correction, for instruction in righteousness: That the man of God may be perfect, throughly furnished unto all good works (2 Timothy 3:16–17).

Part I

A Look at God's Character

.

Chapter 1

God's Immutability and Faithfulness

OUR GOD IS UNCHANGING AND unable to change. What He was for Israel, He still is for us today. On this fact rests all His other attributes. What good would His love or goodness be if He vacillated from one day to the next?

Our God is compared to a rock (Deuteronomy 32:4), an immovable part of nature which remains stable even when the land or sea around it is tumultuous and wind-blown. He is the "Father of lights, with whom is no variableness, neither shadow of turning" (James 1:17). He has not even the slightest hint of changeability!

What a contrast He is to man, who has been described as the "troubled sea, when it cannot rest" (Isaiah 57:20). Even the example of the crowds in the New Testament show man's instability, when the people first exclaimed, "Hosanna to the son of David; Blessed is he that cometh in the name of the Lord" (Matthew 21:9), and then merely a week later they cried out to Pilate, "Let Him be crucified" (Matthew 27:22). The writer of Hebrews sums it up well in the following passage:

For when God made promise to Abraham, because he could swear by no greater, he sware by himself . . . Wherein God, willing more abundantly to shew unto the heirs of promise the immutability of his counsel, confirmed it by an oath: That by two immutable things, in which it was impossible for God to lie, we might have a strong consolation, who have fled for refuge to lay hold upon the hope set before us: Which hope we have as an anchor of the soul, both sure and steadfast (Hebrews 6:13, 17–19).

Our God is immutable in His very essence. Neither His words nor his counsel—extensions of His very being—will ever change; they are established forever, not just in this changing world, but in heaven itself.

The psalmist declares "the counsel of the LORD standeth for ever" (Psalm 33:11), and "for ever, O LORD, thy word is settled in heaven" (Psalm 119:89). God is "I AM that I AM," as He often told Israel. He is, always has been, and always will be ever the same. He says of Himself in Malachi 3:6, "I am the LORD, I change not."

Even Job realized, "He is in one mind, and who can turn him?" (Job 23:13). As A.W. Pink so aptly wrote in *The Attributes of God*, "He cannot change for the better, for He is already perfect; and being perfect, He cannot change for the worse."[1]

God's character, the qualities He portrays, is also unchanging. "His mercy is everlasting; and his truth endureth to all generations" (Psalm 100:5). His kindness and peace will never change: "For the mountains shall depart, and the hills be removed; but my kindness shall not depart from thee, neither shall the covenant of my peace be removed" (Isaiah 54:10). Even His love is unchanging: "I have

---

1   A.W. Pink, *The Attributes of God* (Ann Arbor, Michigan: Bible Truth Depot, 1961), 32.

loved thee with an everlasting love" (Jeremiah 31:3).

Nothing pertaining to God is able to change. He is what He is, and He always will be. His character will always be the same; His works will always be the same. What a comfort this should be to us as His children, knowing the way He led, protected, and provided for His chosen people back in Israel's day is the same way He will lead, protect, and provide for us today—for those who are Jewish by birth as well as those who have been grafted into His chosen family.

Hand-in-hand with God's immutability is His faithfulness. While the term *immutability* pertains mostly to God's very being, the term *faithfulness* relates more to His dealings with man.

Since He is immutable in Himself, He is faithful in everything He does. Faithfulness implies a firm adherence to promises and contracts; it refers to one who is worthy of confidence and belief. Our God firmly adheres to what He is and what He has promised. He is also fully worthy of our trust:

> *God is not a man, that he should lie; neither the son of man, that he should repent: hath he said, and shall he not do it? or hath he not spoken, and shall he not make it good?* (Numbers 23:19)

What a contrast He is to those in the world today—a world filled with countless stories of split marriages, broken vows, destroyed business contracts, and incomplete work. Unfaithfulness is rampant among believers and nonbelievers alike, but we are repeatedly told in Scripture that our God is faithful:

- *Know therefore that the LORD thy God, he is God, the faithful God, which keepeth covenant and mercy with them that love him and keep his commandments to a thousand generations* (Deuteronomy 7:9).

- *God is faithful, by whom ye were called unto the fellowship of his Son Jesus Christ our Lord* (1 Corinthians 1:9).
- *And unto the angel of the church of the Laodiceans write; These things saith the Amen, the faithful and true witness, the beginning of the creation of God* (Revelation 3:14).
- *And I saw heaven opened , and behold a white horse; and he that sat upon him was called Faithful and True, and in righteousness he doth judge and make war* (Revelation 19:11).

Not only are we simply told He is faithful, we are given examples of His faithfulness. The prophet Jeremiah testified of God's adherence to His words when he cried out, "It is of the LORD's mercies that we are not consumed, because his compassions fail not. They are new every morning: great is thy faithfulness" (Lamentations 3:22–23). Abraham's wife, Sarah, trusted God to fulfill the promise of a child when she was well past child-bearing years, "because she judged him faithful who had promised" (Hebrews 11:11).

God is also faithful in meting out punishment when it is deserved. Scripture tells us of the Israelites, who wandered back and forth between theism and paganism for many years. Not only did God remain faithful to take them back as He promised, but He also remained firm in His declaration of punishment when they wandered away from Him.

God's faithfulness even extends to the safe keeping of our very souls. Paul testifies, "I know whom I have believed, and am persuaded that He is able to keep that which I have committed unto Him" (2 Timothy 1:12). We can do so because we know—however we may be tempted or tried—"God is faithful, who will not suffer you to be tempted above that ye are able; but will with the temptation also make a way to escape, that ye may be able to bear it" (1 Corinthians 10:13).

He is consistent in providing salvation and deliverance to His children. He is our "faithful Creator" (1 Peter 4:19) who will do what He has promised to sustain us to the very end.

Chapter 2

God's Knowledge and Wisdom

OUR GOD IS OMNISCIENT; HE is aware of everything. He can never forget anything, nor overlook any piece of information, as man is so wont to do. His knowledge is actually an intricate part of His faithfulness, for it contributes to His ability to adhere to what He has promised.

God's awareness of past, present, and future is infinite and utterly complete. He knows in detail and understands it all. He can never promise anything He cannot fulfill, nor can He make an untrue statement. We must understand the universality of God's knowledge. Every single thing is known by Him:

- *Neither is there any creature that is not manifest in his sight: but all things are naked and opened unto the eyes of him with whom we have to do* (Hebrews 4:13).
- *Great is our Lord, and of great power; his understanding is infinite* (Psalm 147:5).
- *The eyes of the LORD are in every place, beholding the evil and the good* (Proverbs 15:3).

God has knowledge of both wicked and righteous. He is aware of all things taking place in every part of the universe at any given time. Nothing can be hidden from Him.

We see examples of this knowledge throughout Scripture, beginning with Adam and Eve in the Garden of Eden. Though they attempted to hide from God, He knew where they were and why they were hiding. He knew their son Cain murdered his brother Abel, though no human eye had witnessed it. He was aware of Sarah's laughter when she heard Abraham receive the promise of coming child and heir. He knew David's sin with Bathsheba, though David tried to cover it up. He sent the prophet Nathan to David with the message: "your sin will find you out" (Numbers 32:23). In other words, David's sin was not invisible to God; He saw it all.

We see this all-encompassing knowledge even in the New Testament, as Christ met the woman at the well. When He told her to call her husband, she claimed she had no husband. He countered back, "thou hast well said, 'I have no husband.' For thou hast had five husbands; and he whom thou now hast is not thy husband" (John 4:17–18). How could He have known that, unless He had all knowledge?

As we can see, God's knowledge is very personal. As Job declared when contemplating his many afflictions: "he knoweth the way that I take" (Job 23:10). This knowledge extends to us today, in every part of our lives. He, our Creator, knows even the very particles we are made of: "For he knoweth our frame; he remembereth that we are dust" (Psalm 103:14). David expounds upon this complete knowledge in one of his psalms:

O LORD, thou hast searched me and known me. Thou knowest

my downsitting and mine uprising, thou understandest my thought afar off. Thou compassest my path and my lying down, and art acquainted with all my ways. For there is not a word in my tongue, but, lo, O LORD, thou knowest it altogether (Psalm 139:1–4).

As the wise writer wrote so long ago, "a man's heart deviseth his way: but the LORD directeth his steps" (Proverbs 16:9). God knows who we are, of what we are made, and what we can handle. He has known from the beginning which circumstances He will place upon each one of us and has, with each circumstance, known the way of deliverance through or around it. His words in Isaiah are applicable to all of us: "and it shall come to pass, that before they call, I will answer; and while they are yet speaking, I will hear" (Isaiah 65:24).

God's omniscience is also evident in His own plans and prophecies throughout history. As Luke tells us, "known unto God are all His works from the beginning of the world" (Acts 15:18). He has known the end of things from the very beginning, before they even come to pass.

He has known how time will end some day in the future, ever since He created the very beginning of time. He made prophecies about the incarnation and crucifixion of Jesus Christ, and everything happened exactly as He foretold. He has given prophecies about His future return and the glory of our eternal home. His prophecies of old have come to pass; therefore, we can rest assured His plans for the future will happen as well.

God's wisdom is essentially an extension of His omniscience. He has all knowledge of all things; therefore, He has all wisdom.

Wisdom refers to attaining the best possible result by the best possible means. It is the ability to have knowledge and use it correctly. It is the knowledge of circumstances combined with the knowledge of the best way to deal with those circumstances.

Our God is called the "God only wise" (Romans 16:27; 1 Timothy 1:17; Jude 1:25). This capacity of wisdom is peculiar to God alone. He, in essence, *is* wisdom. His wisdom is perfect, constant, and universal. It is utterly beyond human comprehension; yet we know His wisdom exists, for it has been manifested throughout the ages in many circumstances:

- *O Lord, how manifold are thy works! in wisdom hast thou made them all: the earth is full of thy riches* (Psalm 104:24).

- *But of him are ye in Christ Jesus, who of God is made unto us wisdom, and righteousness, and sanctification, and redemption* (1 Corinthians 1:30).

- *O the depth of the riches both of the wisdom and knowledge of God! how unsearchable are his judgments, and his ways past finding out!* (Romans 11:33).

- *With the ancient is wisdom; and in length of days understanding. With him is wisdom and strength, he hath counsel and understanding* (Job 12:12–13).

Our God is infinitely wise. His wisdom has been shown through creation, its perfect harmony, and its intricate detail. It has been shown through the great redemption of mankind. It has been shown through everything in the world around us. It has been shown throughout history and it will be shown through our personal lives.

We can know without a doubt that God knows how to use our

circumstances for our good; He knows what is best for us and how to obtain it. We can rest in the truth of the oft-quoted Romans 8:28, which promises we can "know that all things work together for good to them that love God, to them who are the called according to his purpose." We can rest in its truth because it *is* truth. He is our faithful Creator to whom we can commit the keeping of our souls (1 Peter 4:19). We can trust in Him even when we do not understand our circumstances because He knows and understands, and He knows how bring about a right end to those circumstances.

Chapter 3

God's Goodness

SO, WE HAVE SEEN THAT God has all knowledge and wisdom. Yet how can we fully appreciate this knowledge and wisdom, unless we also believe He is good?

The Psalms repeat numerous times, "the LORD is good and his mercy endureth for ever." Scripture as a whole is full of statements regarding the goodness of our God:

- *O taste and see that the LORD is good: blessed is the man that trusteth in him* (Psalm 34:8).

- *For thou, Lord, art good, and ready to forgive; and plenteous in mercy unto all them that call upon thee* (Psalm 86:5).

- *The LORD is good to all; and his tender mercies are over all his works* (Psalm 145:9).

- *And they sang together in course in praising and giving thanks unto the LORD; because he is good, for his mercy endureth for ever toward Israel* (Ezra 3:11).

- *The LORD is good, a stronghold in the day of trouble; and he knoweth them that trust in him* (Nahum 1:7).

This extolled goodness can also be called kindheartedness, graciousness, benevolence, and cordiality. It is God's desire and tendency to deal bounteously toward His creation. He does what is good for His creation, not for His benefit alone, but also for the creation's well-being.

His goodness is all that indifference is not: He knows, cares, and *does*. In fact, the original Anglo-Saxon meaning of the name *God* is equivalent to *the Good*. He not only does good, He *is* good. He is the only standard of goodness, the ultimate representation of it: "Jesus said unto him, Why callest thou me good? none is good, save one, that is, God" (Luke 18:19).

We see this goodness manifested throughout history—first, in creation itself. We are told "the earth is full of the goodness of the LORD" (Psalm 33:5). God created the world (and mankind) for His own pleasure, but He furnished it richly for man to enjoy. We do not live amidst only those things necessary for our survival.

Think about this for a moment: God created flora and fauna for our enjoyment! He gave us delicious meats and mouth-watering fruits and vegetables. We have a variety of herbs and spices to savor and relish. He gave us birds to musically grace our ears, flowers to delicately enrich the scent of the world around us, and colorful foliage to delight our eyes. He created mankind with five unique senses to enjoy all these things!

God considered His creation of this world to be good: "And God saw every thing that He had made, and, behold, it was very good" (Genesis 1:31). Therefore, we are also to consider His creation to be good: "I will praise thee; for I am fearfully and wonderfully made: marvelous are thy works; and that my soul knoweth right well" (Psalm 139:14).

Second, we see God's goodness in His plan of redemption. He was under no obligation to pity the waywardness of man, or provide a way of escape from man's impending punishment. Yet, He did both.

We are told in Titus 2:11, "the grace of God that bringeth salvation hath appeared to all men." If we look back at the original Greek for this verse, we find the word *grace* is synonymous with the words *goodness* and *benevolence*. It was His goodness which provided a way of salvation from the eternal damnation our sinfulness so rightly deserves.

Paul spells out this work of goodness quite clearly in his letter to the Galatians: "But when the fulness of the time was come, God sent forth his Son, made of a woman, made under the law, to redeem them that were under the law, that we might receive the adoption of sons" (Galatians 4:4–5). He provided redemption and a way for us to be grafted into His family. Why would God do this unless He had "good will toward men" (Luke 2:11)?

Finally, we see the goodness of God in His daily provision for all creation. First, it allows for the preservation of the earth where we live:

> *Thou visitest the earth, and waterest it: thou greatly enrichest it with the river of God, [which] is full of water: thou preparest them corn, when thou hast so provided for it. Thou waterest the ridges thereof abundantly: thou settlest the furrows thereof: thou makest it soft with showers: thou blessest the springing thereof. Thou crownest the year with thy goodness; and thy paths drop fatness* (Psalm 65:9–11).

Not only is God good toward the land He has created, but He is also good toward the creatures inhabiting the land. The psalmist exclaims, "O LORD, thou preservest man and beast" (Psalm 36:6).

His goodness extends beyond man, even to the animals He created. He planned their ability to find food in the wild and survive throughout the seasons without the care of man. He also provides for the plants; for instance, He arrays the lilies of the field in glorious splendor, far more glorious than what Solomon ever wore, even though they "toil not, neither do they spin" (Matthew 6:28).

If God cares so much for those living things unable to know Him as we do, those who will not spend eternity basking in His presence, how dare we think His same goodness does not extend toward us? The whole of Psalm 23 extols His goodness toward man alone, climaxing in verses 5–6: "thou anointest my head with oil; my cup runneth over. Surely goodness and mercy shall follow me all the days of my life: and I will dwell in the house of the LORD for ever."

His goodness is shown to us when He answers our prayers, forgives our sins, helps us with our infirmities, accepts the imperfectness of man, and embraces us as His beloved. Truly, His goodness is boundless and infinite, even as the psalmist exclaims: "the goodness of God endureth continually" (Psalm 52:1).

Chapter 4

God's Loving-Kindness

OUR GOD NOT ONLY LOVES, He *is* love. It is not just one of His many attributes, but rather a part of His very nature. He continually gives of Himself for the benefit of others. The love of God is so often emphasized, and is truly an amazing thing, but do we really understand what His love is?

This section is headed by the more archaic word *loving-kindness* because it seems to most accurately describe God's love as we comprehend it. It is not merely lovey-dovey, feel-good emotional babble. Rather, it is an all-encompassing sacrificial kindness toward man that is regulated by principle: truth supported by action.

The truth of God's love is supported by His preservation of mankind. It is also supported by His correction and testing: "for whom the Lord loveth, He chasteneth" (Hebrews 12:6). Yet, perhaps the greatest proof of His amazing love is the miracle of Calvary:

- *But God commendeth his love toward us, in that, while we were yet sinners, Christ died for us* (Romans 5:8).
- *For God so loved the world, that he gave his only begotten Son, that whosoever believeth in him should not perish, but have everlasting life* (John 3:16).

- *In this was manifested the love God toward us, because that God sent his only begotten son into the world, that we might live through him. Herein is love, not that we loved God, but that he loved us, and sent his son to be the propitiation for our sins* (1 John 4:9–10).

God *so* loved the world—His love goes far beyond any sort of human measurement, any standard we could dare hope to comprehend. This love is infinite; Paul describes it as "the love of Christ, which passeth knowledge" (Ephesians 3:19).

We also know this love is eternal: just as God had no beginning and has no end, so His love has no beginning or end. It has been a part of His very being since before the beginning of time, since the very foundation of the world.

- *The LORD hath appeared of old unto me, saying, Yea, I have loved thee with an everlasting love: therefore with lovingkindness have I drawn thee* (Jeremiah 31:3).

- *Father, I will that they also, whom thou hast given me, be with me where I am; that they may behold my glory, which thou hast given me: for thou lovedst me before the foundation of the world* (John 17:24).

Another amazing thing about God's love, placing it far beyond any comparison, is it is not based upon its object. His love for us is spontaneous, uninfluenced, and free. God loves according to *His* good pleasure:

- *The LORD did not set his love upon you, nor choose you, because ye were more in number than any people; for ye were the fewest of all people* (Deuteronomy 7:7).

- *Who hath saved us, and called us with an holy calling, not according to our works, but according to his own purpose and grace, which was given us in Christ Jesus before the world begin* (2 Timothy 1:9).

- *We love him, because he first loved us* (1 John 4:19).

His love is not based upon anything we could do to merit it. On the contrary, we are far from deserving such kindness and grace. Yet, as His children, we can never be separated from this amazing love—not by physical trials, problems caused by current events, or even spiritual battles.

Who shall separate us from the love of Christ? . . . For I am persuaded, that neither death, nor life, nor angels, nor principalities, nor powers, nor things present, nor things to come, nor height, nor depth, nor any other creature, shall be able to separate us from the love of God, which is in Christ Jesus our Lord (Romans 8:35, 38–39).

The love of God, eternal and incomprehensible, is always with us. It was manifested through the work at Calvary, and will be manifested through our individual lives as we allow it to be. This love is so far beyond what we could ever imagine. Frederick Lehman aptly describes it in his beloved hymn:

The love of God is greater far than tongue or pen can ever tell;
It goes beyond the highest star and reaches to the lowest hell;
The guilty pair, bowed down with care, God gave His Son to win:
His erring child He reconciled and pardoned from his sin.

When years of time shall pass away and earthly thrones and kingdoms fall,
When men, who here refuse to pray, on rocks and hills and

mountains call,
God's love so sure, shall still endure, all measureless and strong:
Redeeming grace to Adam's race—the saints' and angels' song.

Could we with ink the ocean fill and were the skies of parchment
made,
Were ev'ry stalk on earth a quill and ev'ry man a scribe by trade,
To write the love of God above would drain the ocean dry.
Nor could the scroll contain the whole tho stretched from sky to
sky.

O love of God, how rich and pure!
How measureless and strong!
It shall forevermore endure—
The saints' and angels' song.[2]

---

2   Frederick M. Lehman, "The Love of God," *The Hymnal for Worship and Celebration* (Waco, Texas: Word Music, 1986), pt.67.

Chapter 5

God's Sovereignty

WHAT, EXACTLY, IS SOVEREIGNTY? IT combines so many ele-
ments of what makes God who He is: His power over all things, His
wisdom to use this power rightly, His providence and sustenance
each day for His creation, and His ability to use His attributes to
remain actively involved with inanimate and animate parts of His
creation.

He is the Sovereign or the King over all—He ordains and rules
over all. "Our God is in the heavens: he hath done whatsoever he
hath pleased" (Psalm 115:3). He has the unique right to do whatever
He wants. He is "the head of all principality and power" (Colossians
2:10), and He does "all things after the counsel of his own will"
(Ephesians 1:11).

As theologian Charles Hodge explains:

> [Providence] teaches that an infinitely wise, good, and power-
> ful God is everywhere present, controlling all events great and
> small, necessary and free, in a way perfectly consistent with the
> nature of his creatures and with his own infinite excellence, so
> that everything is ordered by his will and is made to subserve

his wise and benevolent designs.[3]

Our God is in control of all things, not just the good but also the seemingly bad. "The LORD maketh poor, and maketh rich: he bringeth low, and lifteth up" (1 Samuel 2:7). He declares: "I, even I, am he, and there is no god with me: I kill, and I make alive; I wound, and I heal: neither is there any that can deliver out of my hand" (Deuteronomy 32:39) . The New Testament repeats this thought: "Therefore hath he mercy on whom he will have mercy, and whom he will he hardeneth" (Romans 9:18).

So, what visible proof do we have of this sovereignty? Where do we see this providence manifested in creation?

First, we are told specifically "by him all things consist" (Colossians 1:17) and "in him we live, and move, and have our being" (Acts 17:28). He not only created all, but He also preserves all. His power alone keeps us in existence. This fact applies not just to man, but to the rest of creation as well—weather, animals, foliage. He created and controls it all, caring for and directing each element, plant, and animal.

- *Whatsoever the LORD pleased, that did he in heaven, and in earth, in the seas, and all deep places. He causeth the vapours to ascend from the ends of the earth; he maketh lightnings for the rain; he bringeth the wind out of his treasuries* (Psalm 135:6–7).

- *God thundereth marvellously with his voice; great things doeth he, which we cannot comprehend. For he saith to the snow, Be thou on the earth; likewise to the small rain, and to the great rain of his strength. He sealeth up the hand of every*

---

*man; that all men may know his work . . . By the breath of
God frost is given: and the breadth of the waters is straitened.
Also by watering he wearieth the thick cloud: he scattereth
his bright cloud: and it is turned round about by his counsels:
that they may do whatsoever he commandeth them upon the
face of the world in the earth* (Job 37:6–12).

- *Behold the fowls of the air: for they sow not, neither do they
reap, nor gather into barns; yet your heavenly Father feedeth
them . . . Consider the lilies of the field, how they grow;
they toil not, neither do they spin: And yet I say unto you,
That even Solomon in all his glory was not arrayed like one
of these* (Matthew 6:26, 28–29).

Of course, if God cares so much for the inanimate and helpless
entities of His creation, how much more do you think He cares for
us, His children, who were created in His very image? This brings
us to our second point regarding God's providence: He leaves nothing to chance or randomness, but rather controls every event enter-
ing our lives.

The book of Job tells us man's "days are determined, the number of his months are with thee, thou hast appointed his bounds that
he cannot pass" (Job 14:5). Indeed, the writer of Proverbs echoes
this sentiment when he tells us "a man's heart deviseth his way: but
the LORD directeth his steps" (Proverbs 16:9), and "man's goings
are of the LORD" (Proverbs 20:24).

God planned out our lives from the beginning of time, and His
hand directs our every step. He controls not only our actions, but
even our emotions and desires: "For it is God which worketh in
you both to will and to do of his good pleasure" (Philippians 2:13).
What a comfort this should be!

C.H. Spurgeon once proclaimed, in a sermon about God's sovereignty:

> *There is no attribute more comforting to His children than the doctrine of Divine Sovereignty. Under the most adverse circumstances, in the most severe troubles, they believe that Sovereignty hath ordained their afflictions, that Sovereignty overrules them, and that Sovereignty will sanctify them all.*[4]

The book of Esther distinctly exhibits this personal providence. Even though God's name is never mentioned in its contents, He was actively directing people and events throughout the entire book. He led the king to call Vashti before him, and then led Vashti to refuse his request. He used those events to lead Esther to the throne as queen. Once Esther claimed the throne, God used her elevation to save His chosen people, the Jews, from total annihilation.

He also guided Haman's hatred of Mordecai, a seemingly unfortunate thing from our point of view. He used this hatred, in conjunction with the king's desire to honor Mordecai, to bring Haman to his demise. Think of it: he was hanged from the very same gallows he had built for Mordecai! Certainly, God controlled and directed the steps of each character in this account.[5]

Finally, we also see His sovereignty is manifested equally—His children, as well as those who have rejected Him, profit alike from this providence. The psalmist states "from the place of his habitation he looketh upon all the inhabitants of the earth. He fashioneth

---

4   C.H. Spurgeon, "Divine Sovereignty" (New Park Street Chapel, Southwark, May 4, 1856).

5   For an expanded study about the personal providence of God, *see also* Layton Talbert, *Not By Chance: Learning to Trust a Sovereign God* (Greenville, South Carolina: BJU Press, 2001).

their hearts alike; he considereth all their works" (Psalm 33:14–15). Also, we are told in the Gospels that "he maketh his sun to rise on the evil and on the good, and sendeth rain on the just and on the unjust" (Matthew 5:45).

Truly, our God has the power to provide for and sustain all His creation. When He appeared to Abraham and Sarah with the promise of a child, He even proclaimed, "Is any thing too hard for the LORD?" (Genesis 18:14). We are reminded of this statement by the prophet Jeremiah's response, "there is nothing too hard for thee" (Jeremiah 32:17).

Again, in the New Testament, we are told countless times that with God, all things are possible. We see through these statements He not only has the *desire* to care for His creation, but He also has the *power* to do so.

We may not understand how He moves and directs. In fact, "as the heavens are higher than the earth, so are my ways higher than your ways, and my thoughts than your thoughts" (Isaiah 55:9). We may not understand His ways, but we can rest in knowing God is King over all. We can rest in His knowledge, and His ability to use this knowledge for our good and His glory. We can sing of His all-encompassing sovereignty, as David did in 1 Chronicles 29:11–12:

> *Thine, O LORD, is the greatness, and the power, and the glory, and the victory, and the majesty: for all that is in the heaven and in the earth is thine; thine is the kingdom, O LORD, and thou art exalted as head above all. Both riches and honour come of thee, and thou reignest over all; and in thine hand is power and might; and in thine hand it is to make great, and to give strength unto all.*

A more modern example of this sovereignty is demonstrated through the life of William Cowper, an eighteenth century hymn-writer. Apparently, after one particularly difficult bout of depression, he had decided to commit suicide. Calling a cab, he told the driver to take him to the Thames River. However, the dangerously thick fog made finding the river impossible. After a while of driving around frustrated, the cab driver eventually stopped and told Cowper to get out.

Surprisingly, they happened to stop directly outside Cowper's home! He went inside and chose not to commit suicide after all. Sometime later, referring directly to this experience, he penned the following words:

God moves in a mysterious way His wonders to perform;
He plants His footsteps in the sea, and rides upon the storm.

Ye fearful saints, fresh courage take; the clouds ye so much dread
Are big with mercy, and shall break in blessings on your head.

Judge not the Lord by feeble sense, but trust Him for His grace;
Behind a frowning providence He hides a smiling face.[6]

---

6   William Cowper, "God Moves in a Mysterious Way," *Worship and Service Hymnal* (Carol Stream, Illinois: Hope Publishing Company, 1973), pt.16.

Chapter 6

Names of God

TO GAIN AN EVEN BETTER understanding of who God is, we must also consider some of the names given to Him throughout Scripture. This section will focus on a few of His names, specifically ones pertaining to our study of sickness and healing.[7]

One of the first names mentioned is *'El Ro'i*: the God who sees. In Genesis 16, we are given the account of Hagar fleeing into the wilderness. Sarah had forced her husband, Abraham, to be sexually intimate with Hagar, and Hagar had success where Sarah had not: she conceived. Naturally, this angered Sarah, and she responded by dealing harshly with Hagar. So Hagar fled into the wilderness to escape the emotional turmoil caused by the whole ordeal.

It was there in the wilderness, the most desolate of places, where the angel of the Lord appeared to Hagar, providing her with instruction for that day and promises for the future. In response, Hagar "called the name of the LORD that spake unto her, Thou God seest me" (Genesis 16:13). Similarly today, He can see us and our needs—physical, emotional, or spiritual.

Another similar name is *Jehovah–jireh*: the God who provides.

7   For further study regarding the names of God, *see also* "God, Names of," *New Bible Dictionary*, 3rd ed. (Downers Grove, IL: InterVarsity Press, 1996).

He not only sees our need, but He also provides a way of fulfillment for that need. In Genesis 22, we read of Abraham leading his only son Isaac up the mountain as a sacrifice in obedience to God's direct command. Abraham obeyed God's command utterly and completely, even to the point of binding his son with ropes and raising the knife to kill him.

However, God—'*El Ro'i*, the God who sees—stopped the action before it could no longer be undone. He called out to Abraham, commending his obedience and directing his attention to a ram caught in the brush nearby. He provided the sacrifice they needed, for if Abraham had slain his son then God's promise that Abraham would be the father of many nations would not have been fulfilled. Abraham offered the ram as his sacrifice to God, instead of his only son Isaac. "And Abraham called the name of that place Jehovah-jireh: as it is said to this day, In the mount of the LORD it shall be seen" (Genesis 22:14).

Another great name of our God is '*El Shaddai*: Lord God Almighty. We have already established He is the supreme Sovereign over all creation. This name also reminds us He will nourish, satisfy, and supply His people with all they need, just as a mother does for her child. He calls Himself by this name when speaking to Abraham and Jacob (Israel), as well as when prophesying to the Apostle John about future events (Revelation 1:8).

Our God is also called '*El 'Elyon*: the Most High God. It is a comparative name, describing the prominence and supreme greatness of God as compared to the rest of creation. This name also denotes His sovereignty, and particularly emphasizes His preeminence over all.

The psalmist uses the word '*elyon* in reference to God when he exclaims, "thou, LORD, art high above all the earth: thou art exalted far above all gods" (Psalm 97:9). Also, God uses this name of Himself when He states, "That they may know from the rising of the sun, and from the west, that there is none beside me. I am the LORD, and there is none else" (Isaiah 45:6). No being or thing can compare to our God!

As the sovereign One who sees all and provides, God can also be called *Jehovah–nissi*: the Lord our Banner. In Exodus 17, we read the account of the Israelites battling against the Amalekites. After God provided a clear victory for Israel, "Moses built an altar, and called the name of it Jehovah–nissi" (Exodus 17:15). Moses was proclaiming that God was the Banner under which they fought; He was the focal point of Israel during that time.

While this is more a commemoration of God's work than an actual name He uses, we can still call upon Him today as our Banner of hope and encouragement. He is the One to whom we should look, not just when engaged in battle—spiritual or otherwise—but every single day. He is to be our focal point as He was for Israel.

Finally, one more name relating directly to our study is *Jehovah–rapha*: the Lord who heals. The Hebrew word *rapha* has several meanings throughout the Old Testament. First, it means to literally repair, as Elijah repaired the altar of the Lord (1 Kings 18:30). Second, it means to purify—after Elisha received the mantle of Elijah, he proved his ability to use God's power by healing (purifying) the waters of the Jordan to no longer cause death or barrenness of the land (2 Kings 2:21). Third, it means to restore to a normal state, such as when God ordered King Abimilech to restore Sarah to her husband, Abraham (Genesis 20:17).

Our God does all these things as the Great Healer, or the Great

Physician: He repairs, purifies, and restores us to a useful state of being. He promises to heal backsliders (Jeremiah 3:22), the wounded (Deuteronomy 32:39), and the spiritually diseased (Psalm 103:3).

Chapter 7

Overview of God's Character

WE HAVE LOOKED AT JUST a few of the characteristics of our God. However, those few provide a strong foundation to define who He is.

- He is absolutely *unchanging*.

- He sees and knows all (*'El Ro'i*), and is utterly wise in using this knowledge for our benefit; this knowledge and wisdom is *unchanging*.

- He is wholly good; there is not one part of God that is not good. This goodness is *unchanging*.

- He loves us unconditionally and eternally. This love is *unchanging*.

- He is altogether sovereign (*'El Shaddai, 'El 'Elyon*); He directs and provides daily for His entire creation (*Jehovah-jireh*). This sovereignty or providence is also *unchanging*.

- He is the God upon whom we can call in any circumstance. His names establish His reputation. His reputation is *unchanging.*

Although we will never have a perfect knowledge of God until we reach heaven, we ought to study and meditate upon these characteristics until we can recognize them in our everyday circumstances. Careful study of the Word of God can teach us how to recognize these attributes. We can read through the Psalms to note how He is praised and described. We can read through the historical books of the Bible to see how He has acted throughout the ages. We can read through the prophecies to see how He promises to act in the future.

Hymnals are also filled with proclamations of our God's character. The authors of those songs had an intimate knowledge of God, which could only have come through personal experience.

Take some time to look through one; meditate on songs such as "Great is Thy Faithfulness;" "Our Great Saviour;" "He Giveth More Grace;" "The Love of God;" "Master, the Tempest is Raging;" "O God, Our Help in Ages Past;" "O Worship the King;" or "Immortal, Invisible, God Only Wise."

Of course, all this study can in no way compare to a consistent personal walk with God. Knowing and walking with Him daily teaches us His character better than anything else. While it is necessary to study the Bible and meditate upon its words—and while it is ever so helpful to think on the words penned by hymn-writers through the ages—head knowledge alone cannot save us.

Heart knowledge, however, comes from a personal relationship with God. This same heart knowledge will teach us, in a very real way, who our God is and how He relates to us.

Part II

A Look at God's Works

Chapter 8

Ministry on Earth

WHILE CHRIST'S MAIN OBJECTIVE IN coming to earth was to redeem mankind for eternity, He also provided many other ministries
to the men and women of that day. We want to look specifically
at His ministry of healing, both in the physical realm—casting out
disease—as well as the spiritual—casting out demons. These healings give us an idea of His compassionate nature toward us, and
His ability to heal all our diseases. They also give us an idea of the
differences among various healings.[8]

One of the first recorded instances of someone being healed
by Christ is Peter's mother-in-law. In fact, three out of the four
Gospels share this miracle with us (Matthew 8:14–15, Mark 1:29–31,
Luke 4:38–39). Luke tells us Christ "rebuked the fever; and it left
her," proving by the fever's obedience, *He has authority over physical
disease.*

In addition, not only did the fever break, but "immediately she
arose and ministered unto them." In other words, the healing was
absolute and complete; she had no lingering effects!

Another aspect of Christ's healing power is shown as He cast out

---

8   *See also* Appendix A: "Healings Performed during Christ's Earthly Ministry."

demons. Mark 1:34 records one such instance, telling how Christ forbade the demons to speak "because they knew him." Clearly, *He has authority over spiritual disease* (demons) as well as physical.

Later in the same chapter, a leper approaches Christ for healing, proving yet another aspect of His power (Mark 1:40–42). Even today, leprosy does not have an established cure. Yet Christ provided full healing for the man, demonstrating His authority over *all* diseases, even those without known cures.

In the next chapter of Mark, we find the account of the paralytic man whose friends brought him before Christ to be healed. Before providing physical healing for the man, Christ first grants forgiveness for his sins. The order of His actions and words is significant. Disease came into the world as a result of sin. Thus, by first forgiving the man's sins, He healed the ultimate cause of the sickness. He then went on to heal the consequence of sin in the man's body (paralysis). His healing was complete, since the man was able to freely walk away from the house as soon as Christ spoke the words (Mark 2:3–12).

Another incident in Mark reveals that His healing restores usefulness. Mark 3:1–5 tells of the man with a withered hand, resulting from either disease or accident. This man was obviously disabled, and probably unable to work for a living. He needed the constant assistance of others in his life.

Before the man could be healed, however, the nearby Pharisees and Herodians accused Christ of breaking the Sabbath by doing work on that day. He countered their accusation with a typical question, asking if it was lawful to do good on the Sabbath. He also asked whether they should save a life or—by not working—essentially kill it. As usual, the Jewish leaders had no answer for Christ, and He went on to do the good work of healing. He commanded the man to stretch out his hand, and restored it to a normal, useful state, so the man could once again work and provide for himself.

Going on to the next few verses, we see Christ healing a multitude of men and women (Mark 3:7–12). In this instance, at least, His healing was all-inclusive: He helped everyone who came to Him. They knew of Christ's reputation and, desperately wanting restoration, they came to Him so eagerly that His disciples had to prepare a ship for Him to escape the thronging and pressing of the crowds. Yet, despite the intensity and diversity of the crowds, He healed all who came to Him.

We are not told of Him turning away anyone in the multitudes—no matter how sick or demon-possessed the person was, no matter how old or young, proud or humble, believing or unbelieving. However, Christ did not always heal all who were present. Sometimes He chose to withdraw from the multitude rather than provide healing to the entire multitude (Luke 5:15–16, John 5:1–13).

Moving on to another aspect of Christ's healings, we find He heals in His own way. Mark 7:31–37 tells of a man who was deaf and dumb. Whoever brought this man to Christ requested He lay His hands upon the man to heal him. However, Christ did not heal in the simple way requested. Rather, He took the man aside and used multiple outward actions to provide healing.

We also see this portrayed in the next chapter of Mark, when a blind man is brought to Christ for healing. Again, instead of simply laying His hands on the man and restoring his sight, He chose to provide a more gradual restoration of sight. His healings are not bound by man's rules or guidelines.

Luke's gospel offers a few more characteristics of Christ's earthly ministry of healing. One particular instance clearly shows us His healing power comes from God alone. In Luke 11:14–26, we read another account of a mute, demon-possessed man. We are not told whether this man came to Christ independently or was brought by friends. However, once again Christ provided physical and spiritual healing. He then admonished the onlookers who doubted His authority, "a house divided against a house falleth." In other words, why or how could Satan cast out one of his own? The devil would not use his powers against himself. Thus, His power to heal comes from God alone.

Finally, John 4:46–54 tells of a nobleman whose son was sick unto death. The man approached Christ on the road to Galilee, and urgently begged for his son's healing. Christ tested the nobleman, suggesting he would need signs and wonders in order to believe. However, the nobleman persisted in his entreaty. He had faith to take Christ at His word; he required no outward evidence of fact, but simply believed Christ would heal his son. Christ finally healed the son simply by speaking: "Go thy way, thy son liveth." His healings always involve our faith.

Through all of these examples, we see the diverse aspects of Christ's healings on earth. First, we recognize the vast array of illnesses Christ healed: "the blind receive their sight, and the lame walk, the lepers are cleansed, and the deaf hear, the dead are raised up, and the poor have the gospel preached to them" (Matthew 11:4–5).

Second, as we see through these healings, Christ was often "moved with compassion" towards mankind (Matthew 9:36; Mark 1:41; Mark 6:34; Luke 7:12–13). He did not turn away anyone who sought His healing. Rather, He healed and restored them to their individual states of usefulness.

Third, we see His deity. According to Luke 4:18, His ministry fulfilled the prophecy of Isaiah 61:1–2: "The Spirit of the Lord is upon me, because he hath anointed me to preach the gospel to the poor; he hath sent me to heal the brokenhearted, to preach deliverance to the captives, and recovering of sight to the blind, to set at liberty them that are bruised." Although Christ's main objective in coming to earth was to save mankind from sin's eternal punishment, He provided this ministry of healing as a way to establish His authority and authenticity as the promised Messiah.

Remember the paralytic man who was lowered down through the roof? Christ restored the man's physical health as a sign that He had also restored the man's spiritual health. He healed the paralysis as proof He had forgiven the man's sins.

All of His healings, and all of His other ministries on earth, point clearly to the main reason for His incarnation: the work of atonement.

Chapter 9

Work of Atonement

HAVING CONSIDERED CHRIST'S HEALING MINISTRY here on earth, we can now move on to His main reason for becoming man: His work of atonement for all mankind. Let us examine what exactly what the atonement is—its definition, purpose, provisions, and nature.

Consider some basic definitions of the word atonement. Bible dictionaries and concordances provide several variances of the word and some fundamental interpretations of this work of Christ. The word *atonement* can refer to a cleansing or covering for sin, an expiation or satisfaction for sin's wages, a reconciliation between an offender (man) and an offended one (God), or a restoration to favor with God.

More specifically, this atonement speaks of Christ's death on the cross, and the power of His death and bloodshed to save men from eternal separation from God. So, why do we need this atonement?

First, man is estranged from God and requires a Savior to restore his broken relationship. According to Romans 3:23, "all have sinned and come short of the glory of God." Romans 5:12 clarifies the origin of that sin nature: "Wherefore, as by one man sin entered into the world, and death by sin; and so death passed upon all men, for that all have sinned." All humanity is born with a sin nature, and as Romans 6:23 tells us, we are all condemned to death for that sin. We can do absolutely nothing on our own to merit the favor of God for salvation.

Second, God's very nature demands atonement for our sin. He is wholly righteous, "a God of truth and without iniquity, just and right is he" (Deuteronomy 32:4). God, in His righteousness and holiness, finds it impossible to ignore His laws or the consequences of disobeying those laws.

We need only to observe Israel, who continuously chose to ignore God and follow after idols, to see this righteousness displayed. Each time Israel forsook God's laws, He faithfully sent the promised consequences of their rebellion. They had to pay the price for their sins, before communication could be restored. Thus, we have a twofold need for Christ's atonement: the plight of man and the nature of God.

Moving on to the provisions of the atonement, there are five basic aspects we must consider. These are: cleansing, substitution, redemption, reconciliation, and propitiation.

First, the atonement provides cleansing. "The blood of Jesus Christ his Son cleanseth us from all sin" (1 John 1:7). Through Christ's substitutionary death on the cross, we can be washed clean of any hint of sin and presented as pure before God the Father.

Second, the atonement provides a substitution for sinners. "God commendeth [made known] his love toward us, in that, while we were yet sinners, Christ died for us" (Romans 5:8).

In order to understand the last two words of this verse, we must look to the Old Testament law, which provides us with the foundations of the atonement by describing the requirements for offering sacrifices: "For the life of the flesh is in the blood: and I have given it to you upon the altar to make an atonement for your souls: for it is the blood that maketh an atonement for the soul" (Leviticus 17:11). This is reiterated in the New Testament: "without shedding of blood is no remission [forgiveness]" (Hebrews 9:22). The Law required these sacrifices to be wholly pure, or "without blemish" (Exodus 12:5; Numbers 6:14, 28:3).

Throughout the Old Testament, high priests would sacrifice these spotless animals as substitutions for their own sins and for the sins of their people. However, these sacrifices had to be offered repeatedly, and they only atoned for the ones actively involved in the sacrifice—those who provided the animal, or performed the sacrifice. Therefore, they could never provide a perfect or lasting payment for man's sin.

Yet, Christ came to earth "to give his life a ransom for many" (Mark 10:45). He came as the perfect and wholly obedient Lamb of God, who was "obedient unto death, even the death of the cross" (Philippians 2:8). He provided through His death a permanent atonement, or substitution, for *all* of mankind.

Third, the atonement offers redemption, specifically from sin. This refers to a ransom or freedom that comes from a payment being made.

The book of Ruth provides a picture of what redemption commonly meant in the Old Testament: the buying back of one in distress by a kinsman-redeemer, usually a close male relative. In the narrative given to us, we see Boaz literally buying back or redeeming Ruth, his close relative, to provide her with freedom from her distress. In the same way, Christ's death redeems us from the distress of sin.

Galatians 3:10 establishes our distress as sinners: "For as many as are of the works of the law are under the curse." However, we are freed from such condemnation by Christ's payment on the cross: "Christ hath redeemed us from the curse of the law, being made a curse for us: for it is written, Cursed is every one that hangeth on a tree" (Galatians 3:13). We have been redeemed "with the precious blood of Christ, as of a lamb without blemish and without spot" (1 Peter 1:19). This redemption provides freedom *from* the curse of the law and bondage of sin, freedom *through* the blood of Jesus Christ, and freedom *to* eternal life in Christ and with the Father.[9]

Fourth, the atonement provides a way of reconciliation between God and man. Romans 5:6–10 describes mankind as being ungodly, sinful, and hostile toward God. Our fellowship with God was broken completely. Yet, while in this broken state, we were "reconciled to God by the death of His son."

Most of us know John 3:16—"For God so loved the world, that he gave his only begotten Son, that whosoever believeth in him should not perish, but have everlasting life." We can be reconciled to God through His Son. Our sin natures can be transformed into something new, compatible with the holiness of God, and we can be "made the righteousness of God" (2 Corinthians 5:17–21). Through the atonement, our fellowship with God can be restored, and our relationship changed from one of hostility to one of harmony.

Fifth, the work of the atonement provides a propitiation for sins.

---

9   This does not mean we will never sin; rather, we now have the freedom to choose righteousness instead of sinfulness (*see* Romans 8).

As the perfect Lamb of God, Christ was the only offering which could fully satisfy the wrath of God.

His suffering on the cross entailed great physical torment, as He was tortured and executed in one of the most excruciating ways to die. Even more, He suffered infinite spiritual anguish. God the Father, from whom He had never known separation, actually turned His back on His only Son. As Christ took upon Himself the sins of the whole world—every sin, of every person, at every point in time—God became miraculously estranged from Himself.

Along with the marring of His holiness, and breaking of His perfect union with His Father, He was required to face the complete wrath of His Father, the ultimate punishment for sin. Truly, "herein is love, not that we loved God, but that he loved us, and sent his Son to be the propitiation for our sins" (1 John 4:10), and "not for ours only, but also for the sins of the whole world" (1 John 2:2). He suffered once for our sins, so we do not have to suffer eternally!

God, in His compassionate and merciful nature, was moved by man's desperate plight. He chose to provide the ultimate sacrifice to pay the price for our sins: His only Son. "God commendeth [made known] his love toward us, in that, while we were yet sinners, Christ died for us" (Romans 5:8). Thus, the atonement, or Christ's death on the cross, provided a way for man to be cleansed from the stain of sin. Man was forgiven the requirement of sin's sacrifice, freed from the punishment of sin, and transformed from the hostility of sin as it permanently satisfied the wrath of God.

We must pause here to consider how the atonement relates to our study of physical healing, and whether or not it offers physical benefits as well as spiritual. In prophesying the Messiah's death on the cross, Isaiah 53:4–5 states: "He hath borne our griefs and carried our sorrows . . . by whose stripes ye are healed." This phrase is reiterated in the New Testament (Matthew 8:16–17; 1 Peter 2:24).

Some would interpret these passages to mean Christ's death on the cross eliminated not only the problem of sin, but also its consequences, including physical sickness. However, the immediate removal of sickness is not a guarantee provided with the atonement. In fact, if physical healing was provided through the atonement, how then did Christ provide healing for so many during His ministry on earth *before* His death on the cross?

We can better understand this by using biblical hermeneutics, which provide the basic principles of biblical interpretation. These principles guide us in interpreting the Scriptures reverentially (all Scripture is given by God), grammatically (the meaning of specific words), historically (providing social and cultural background), literarily (distinguishing between literal and figurative or symbolic), and coherently (all Scripture is in harmony with itself).

Hermeneutical principles also emphasize the significance of the context surrounding a specific verse, and the literality and simplicity of Scripture. In other words, the simplest, clearest, and most literal meaning of a passage is often the best way to interpret it, without any double meanings or innuendos.[10] By following these principles, using various study tools available (such as commentaries and Bible dictionaries), and being guided by the Holy Spirit, almost any believer can properly understand Scripture and accurately apply it.

Specifically regarding the question of physical healing through

---

10   For more information on the study of hermeneutics, *see* Stewart Custer, "Part II: The Use of Tools," *Tools for Teaching and Preaching the Bible* (Greenville, South Carolina: Bob Jones University Press, 1998); and Robertson McQuilken, *Understanding and Applying the Bible* (Chicago: Moody Press, 1992).

the atonement, we must consider the context of the given passages (Isaiah 53:4–5; Matthew 8:16–17; 1 Peter 2:24). Although each passage refers to being healed by Christ's death, not one of the surrounding contexts even mentions physical sickness. Rather, they center quite clearly on spiritual sickness (sin). Taking the verses at face-value and rejecting any thought of hidden meanings, as the principle of literality dictates, we must conclude Christ's death provides immediate freedom from spiritual disease alone.

However, we do find other areas of Scripture promising believers future freedom from physical sickness, as we will discover in this next section.

Chapter 10

Promise of Glorification

THIS FUTURE FREEDOM FROM PHYSICAL suffering is brought to us through the promise of glorification, a promise of manifold transformation spiritually and physically. The word *glorification* stems from the word *glory*—a concept similar to splendor, wealth, triumph, and magnificence.

Scripture frequently proclaims the glory of God and His magnificence. It speaks of the glory of Christ's coming, the triumph of His return, and the wealth of splendor that will accompany Him. In a similar manner, we will one day experience this glory in our bodies and spirits. By Christ's triumph over sin, we will be dramatically transformed into something magnificent and glorious.

There are several aspects to this amazing promise of glorification. First, we will be made spiritually perfect. Our sanctification—the process of becoming Christ-like which begins at the moment of salvation—will be complete. We will experience the removal of all sin and temptation, enabling us to finally be "holy and without blame" before God the Father (Ephesians 1:4).

In addition, we will receive all fullness of knowledge. Paul says of that future day, "then shall I know even as also I am known" (1

Corinthians 13:12). John declares, "when he shall appear, we shall be like him; for we shall see him as he is" (1 John 3:2). We will no longer need to rely on secondhand accounts given to us within Scripture, for we will have personal face-to-face knowledge of God and His glory!

Finally, the key thought which correlates with this study: we will experience complete physical transformation. Our bodies will be drastically changed from a state of humiliation to a state of glory.

Romans 8:17–30 particularly establishes this doctrine.

> *And if children, then heirs; heirs of God, and joint-heirs with Christ; if so be that we suffer with him, that we may be also glorified together . . . Moreover whom he did predestinate, them he also called: and whom he called, them he also justified: and whom he justified, them he also glorified.*

As children of God, we will experience both suffering and glory. Regarding our suffering, Paul says we "groan within ourselves, waiting for the adoption, to wit, the redemption of our body" (Romans 8:23; *see also* 2 Corinthians 5:2). We groan as intensely as a woman in childbirth for our bodies to be redeemed (bought back) from sin's power!

Yet, "our light affliction, which is but for a moment, worketh for us a far more exceeding and eternal weight of glory" (2 Corinthians 4:17). We may groan under the weight of present suffering, but our future glorification far exceeds anything we experience in this world! "The sufferings of this present time are not worthy to be compared with the glory which shall be revealed in us" (Romans 8:18).

What exactly is this glory, this redemption of our bodies? According to Philippians 3:21, Christ will "change our vile body, that it may be fashioned like unto his glorious body." He will literally transform the substance of our sin-filled, mortal flesh to be like His perfect, immortal body. We will be changed from corruption (death) to incorruption (eternal life), brokenness to glory, and physical weakness to spiritual power.

This glorification is not a process which begins in this lifetime. Rather, it is a one-time event: "In a moment, in the twinkling of an eye, at the last trump: for the trumpet shall sound, and the dead shall be raised incorruptible, and we shall be changed" (1 Corinthians 15:52). We will be instantly transformed!

We may suffer for a while here on earth, but our future with Christ will be gloriously free from affliction. Our bodies and spirits will be transformed, and we will see God as He is—for we will be like Him.

> *Behold, the tabernacle of God is with men, and he will dwell with them, and they shall be his people, and God himself shall be with them, and be their God. And God shall wipe away all tears from their eyes; and there shall be no more death, neither sorrow, nor crying, neither shall there be any more pain: for the former things are passed away* (Revelation 21:3–4).

Part III

A Look at Our Circumstances

Chapter 11

Certainty of Suffering

WE HAVE SEEN WHO OUR God is, how He has worked in the past, and what He promises to do in the future. With these truths in mind, we can now turn our gaze from vertical to horizontal, and start to consider our circumstances.

In doing so, we must recognize God has a definite plan for every single one of His children, and affliction—physical or otherwise—is a certain part of that plan. Scripture clearly establishes this truth.

- *My son, despise not the chastening of the LORD; neither be weary of his correction: for whom the LORD loveth he correcteth; even as a father the son in whom he delighteth* (Proverbs 3:11–12).

- *In the world ye shall have tribulation: but be of good cheer; I have overcome the world* (John 16:33).

- *For unto you it is given in the behalf of Christ, not only to believe on him, but also to suffer for his sake* (Philippians 1:29).

Scripture also provides us with many examples of those who suffered great afflictions, confirming God's children will face trouble in this life. We read of the prophets, "who have spoken in the name of the Lord, for an example of suffering affliction, and of patience" (James 5:10). We also read of the apostles facing intense physical suffering:

> *We are troubled on every side, yet not distressed; we are perplexed, but not in despair; persecuted, but not forsaken; cast down, but not destroyed; always bearing about in the body the dying of the Lord Jesus, that the life also of Jesus might be made manifest in our body* (2 Corinthians 4:8–10).

For most of us, however, it is not enough to simply know we will suffer here on earth. We want to know *where* suffering comes from and *why* we must face it in our lifetimes. We want to know what good can come from it.

Even as we study through these things, we must keep in the forefront of our minds what we have just seen concerning the character and works of our God. Only by focusing on God first and foremost can we accurately begin to comprehend His ways in our lives.

Chapter 12

Origins of Suffering

THE FIRST QUESTION WE NEED to consider is where our suffering originates. Does it come from God? Is it from Satan? Do we bring it upon ourselves? To determine the answer, we must consider not only what is clearly stated in Scripture, but also the myriad of examples shared throughout the Word of people who suffered physically.

There are several instances throughout Scripture where Satan appears to be the source of sickness. Perhaps the most well-known example is found in the record of Job:

> *Again there was a day when the sons of God came to present themselves before the LORD, and Satan came also among them to present himself before the LORD. And the LORD said unto Satan, From whence comest thou? And Satan answered the LORD, and said, From going to and fro in the earth, and from walking up and down in it. And the LORD said unto Satan, Hast thou considered my servant Job, that there is none like him in the earth, a perfect and an upright man, one that feareth God, and escheweth evil? and still he holdeth fast his integrity, although thou movedst me against him, to destroy him without cause. And*

Satan answered the LORD, and said, Skin for skin, yea, all that a man hath will he give for his life. But put forth thine hand now, and touch his bone and his flesh, and he will curse thee to thy face. And the LORD said unto Satan, Behold, he is in thine hand; but save his life (Job 2:1–6).

We read similar accounts in the Gospels. Luke 13:16 tells us about Christ healing a woman who was "a daughter of Abraham, whom Satan hath bound, lo, these eighteen years." Yet, although Satan seems to be the origin of some physical suffering, he is always subject to God's authority. He can do nothing without God's permission.

Of course, the majority of examples throughout Scripture clearly recognize God as the actual source of our physical infirmities. He is the great Creator of all, as He reminded Moses from the burning bush: "And the LORD said unto him, Who hath made man's mouth? or who maketh the dumb, or deaf, or the seeing, or the blind? have not I the LORD?" (Exodus 4:11).

As Creator, He has the right to do whatever He wants with His creation, even if that includes inflicting severe illness or allowing death. We see this sovereign right exercised throughout the Old and New Testaments:

- *And while the flesh was yet between their teeth, ere it was chewed, the wrath of the LORD was kindled against the people, and the LORD smote the people with a very great plague* (Numbers 11:33).
- *And it came to pass about ten days after, that the LORD smote Nabal, that he died* (1 Samuel 25:38).
- *And the LORD struck the child that Uriah's wife bare unto*

David, and it was very sick (2 Samuel 12:15).

- *And the LORD smote the king, so that he was a leper unto the day of his death, and dwelt in a several house* (2 Kings 15:5; 2 Chronicles 26:20).

- *Neither did Jeroboam recover strength again in the days of Abijah: and the LORD struck him, and he died* (2 Chronicles 13:20).

- *And immediately the angel of the Lord smote him [Herod], because he gave not God the glory: and he was eaten of worms, and gave up the ghost* (Acts 12:23).

God has ultimate authority over all things, including affliction. He alone gives Satan the power to harm our flesh. He alone allows sin's consequences to ravage our bodies. Nothing—not a simple cold or a rare disease—can happen without His permission.

Chapter 13

Purposes of Physical Suffering

KNOWING OUR SUFFERING IS FULLY under God's authority, we can now observe some specific reasons why He allows us, even ordains us, to suffer. For the purpose of this book, we will focus on passages specifically related to physical suffering.[11]

As humans, we have a limited view of suffering in this world. However, we should recall the words spoken to the prophet Isaiah: "For as the heavens are higher than the earth, so are my ways higher than your ways, and my thoughts than your thoughts" (Isaiah 55:9). We must remember God's admonition to Job in the midst of his tribulation:

> *Where wast thou when I laid the foundations of the earth? declare, if thou hast understanding . . . Hast thou entered into the springs of the sea? or hast thou walked in the search of the depth? Have the gates of death been opened unto thee? or hast thou seen the doors of the shadow of death? Hast thou perceived the breadth of the earth? declare if thou knowest it all* (Job 38:4, 16–18).

---

11 *See also* Appendix B: "General Purposes of Trials."

In other words, if we cannot know and describe in full all the intricacies of creation, how can we completely understand the reasons behind it all? As author Edith Schaeffer questions in her book, *Affliction*: "If you can't understand these things, then do you not recognize that you are not full of enough knowledge to comprehend all that is happening to you at this moment of history?"[12] Yet, even though we cannot fully comprehend God's ways, He has provided us with His Word which, in turn, provides us with many clearly stated reasons for physical affliction.

One of the most frequently recognized reasons for physical suffering is chastisement for sin: "whom the Lord loveth he chasteneth, and scourgeth every son whom he receiveth" (Hebrews 12:6). This is what Job's friends suggested as the cause for his affliction, although they were wrong in their conclusion as we see through God's response to Job's cry, and this is what many people first consider when wondering why they are suffering.

Many Scripture passages support this reasoning. For example, the first chapter of Isaiah portrays God's chastisement upon Israel for their rebellion:

> *Ah sinful nation, a people laden with iniquity, a seed of evildoers, children that are corrupters: they have forsaken the LORD, they have provoked the Holy One of Israel unto anger, they are gone away backward. Why should ye be stricken any more? ye will revolt more and more: the whole head is sick, and the whole heart faint. From the sole of the foot even unto the head there is no soundness in it; but wounds, and bruises, and putrifying sores: they have not been closed, neither bound up, neither mollified*

---

12 Edith Schaeffer, *Affliction* (Old Tappan, New Jersey: Fleming H. Revell Company, 1978), 57.

with ointment (Isaiah 1:5–6).

Because Israel had forsaken God and provoked Him to anger, they were stricken with sores and weakness. In other words, they were spiritually flogged for their rebellion.

Another clear portrayal of God's chastisement is found in Psalm 38, when David cries out for mercy from the Lord:

> *For mine iniquities are gone over mine head: as an heavy burden they are too heavy for me. My wounds stink and are corrupt because of my foolishness. I am troubled; I am bowed down greatly; I go mourning all the day long. For my loins are filled with a loathsome disease: and there is no soundness in my flesh. I am feeble and sore broken: I have roared by reason of the disquietness of my heart* (Psalm 38:4–8).

Several New Testament passages also mention sin as the root cause of some physical afflictions, even of death itself. Consider Paul's words concerning those who observe the Lord's Supper:

> *For he that eateth and drinketh unworthily, eateth and drinketh damnation to himself, not discerning the Lord's body. For this cause many are weak and sickly among you, and many sleep* (1 Corinthians 11:29–30).

However, sin is not the only cause of physical suffering. It can also be the result of natural causes, the simple consequence of our imperfect human nature.

Old and New Testament passages support this correlation. For instance, Daniel 8 describes a vision and its interpretation, given by God to Daniel. It records how this event affected Daniel physically: "And I Daniel fainted, and was sick certain days; afterward I rose up, and did the king's business" (Daniel 8:27).

In the New Testament, Paul's letter to the Philippians describes the suffering of Epaphroditus, who simply over-worked himself to the point of illness: "For indeed he was sick nigh unto death . . . for the work of Christ he was nigh unto death, not regarding his life, to supply your lack of service toward me" (Philippians 2:27, 30).We also read about Timothy, who was instructed to "use a little wine for . . . thine often infirmities" (1 Timothy 5:23). We are not told his infirmities were caused by any specific sin; they simply resulted from the vulnerability and finiteness of human flesh.

Of course, even when sickness is merely due to the degeneration of our bodies, the degeneration is ultimately caused by our sin nature. When Adam and Eve sinned in the Garden of Eden, mankind was transformed from perfection and immortality to imperfection and mortality: "Wherefore, as by one man sin entered into the world, and death by sin; and so death passed upon all men, for that all have sinned" (Romans 5:12). Suddenly, sin began destroying man's body.

In addition to specific sins and the consequences of having a sin nature, Scripture records yet another cause for suffering: satanic opposition. While no child of God can be possessed by Satan or his demons, they can still oppose and attack us. In fact, the book of Peter tells us the devil prowls like a "roaring lion . . . seeking whom he may devour" (1 Peter 5:8). He frequently seeks permission from God to afflict us, to cause us to stumble or doubt God. "Satan answered the LORD, and said, Skin for skin, yea, all that a man hath will he give for his life. But put forth thine hand now, and touch his bone and his flesh, and he will curse thee to thy face" (Job 2:4–5).

This leads to a fourth reason for physical suffering: spiritual enrichment. David refers to this several times throughout the Psalms: "Before I was afflicted I went astray: but now have I kept thy word . . . It is good for me that I have been afflicted; that I might learn thy statutes" (Psalm 119:67, 71). Hebrews 12 develops the idea further, adding that such affliction is actually a mark of God's favor toward us.

> *For whom the Lord loveth he chasteneth, and scourgeth every son whom he receiveth If ye endure chastening, God dealeth with you as with sons; for what son is he whom the father chasteneth not? But if ye be without chastisement, whereof all are partakers, then are ye bastards, and not sons. Furthermore we have had fathers of our flesh which corrected us, and we gave them reverence: shall we not much rather be in subjection unto the Father of spirits, and live? For they verily for a few days chastened us after their own pleasure; but he for our profit, that we might be partakers of his holiness. Now no chastening for the present seemeth to be joyous, but grievous: nevertheless afterward it yieldeth the peaceable fruit of righteousness unto them which are exercised thereby* (Hebrews 12:6–11).

In addition to these passages, Paul's letter to the Corinthians suggests another form of spiritual enrichment: receiving divine comfort. As God comforts us through our afflictions, we are thereby equipped to extend the same comfort to others in their affliction (2 Corinthians 1:3–4). Suffering seems to be the most effective way to truly learn the art of giving comfort.

Of course, if we are able to grow spiritually through our physical affliction, or help others grow spiritually, we will further glorify God. This is yet another reason for suffering articulated throughout Scripture.

- *And as Jesus passed by, he saw a man which was blind from his birth. And his disciples asked him, saying, Master, who did sin, this man, or his parents, that he was born blind? Jesus answered, Neither hath this man sinned, nor his parents: but that the works of God should be made manifest in him* (John 9:1–3).

- *Now a certain man was sick, named Lazarus, of Bethany, the town of Mary and her sister Martha ... Therefore his sisters sent unto him, saying, Lord, behold, he whom thou lovest is sick. When Jesus heard that, he said, This sickness is not unto death, but for the glory of God, that the Son of God might be glorified thereby* (John 11:1, 3–4).

- *And lest I should be exalted above measure through the abundance of the revelations, there was given to me a thorn in the flesh, the messenger of Satan to buffet me, lest I should be exalted above measure. For this thing I besought the Lord thrice, that it might depart from me. And he said unto me, My grace is sufficient for thee: for my strength is made perfect in weakness. Most gladly therefore will I rather glory in my infirmities, that the power of Christ may rest upon me* (2 Corinthians 12:7–9).

Finally, Scripture records the lives of many prophets who endured horrible afflictions as examples "of suffering affliction, and of patience" (James 5:10). Hebrews 11 also shares many examples of prophets and disciples who suffered physical tribulation because of their unwavering confidence in God and His promises, men and women who are later named "so great a cloud of witnesses" (Hebrews 12:1).

These examples were given to us so we might learn from them. By regarding their reasons for and responses to suffering, we can learn how to respond to our own suffering.

Chapter 14

Examples of Physical Suffering

GOD'S WORD CONTAINS MANY ACCOUNTS of those who faced physical affliction. Regardless of why each individual suffered, it helps to know there are others who have gone before us. It is encouraging to know others have dealt with the same afflictions we face today.

Consider these Old Testament examples:

- *And it came to pass, that when Isaac was old, and his eyes were dim, so that he could not see (Genesis 27:1).*

- *And when he saw that he prevailed not against him, he touched the hollow of his thigh; and the hollow of Jacob's thigh was out of joint, as he wrestled with him ... And as he passed over Penuel the sun rose upon him, and he halted upon his thigh (Genesis 32:25, 31).*

- *Now Elisha was fallen sick of his sickness whereof he died ... And Elisha died, and they buried him (2 Kings 13:14, 20).*

- *So went Satan forth from the presence of the LORD, and smote Job with sore boils from the sole of his foot unto his crown. And he took him a potsherd to scrape himself withal; and he sat down among the ashes (Job 2:7–8).*

- *I am weary with my groaning; all the night make I my bed to swim; I water my couch with my tears (Psalm 6:6).*
- *And I Daniel fainted, and was sick certain days* (Daniel 8:27).

The Gospels are also rich with examples, telling of multitudes who were afflicted physically in myriad ways. Christ never condemned any of them for being sick; rather, He showed them great mercy:

And great multitudes came unto him, having with them those that were lame, blind, dumb, maimed, and many others, and cast them down at Jesus' feet; and he healed them (Matthew 15:30).

Of course, no list of examples would be complete without the Apostle Paul, who suffered countless trials after his conversion to Christianity. He wrote often of having difficulty with his eyes, an unspecified "thorn in the flesh," and a whole list of other tribulations.

- *And lest I should be exalted above measure through the abundance of the revelations, there was given to me a thorn in the flesh, the messenger of Satan to buffet me, lest I should be exalted above measure* (1 Corinthians 12:7).
- *Of the Jews five times received I forty stripes save one. Thrice was I beaten with rods, once was I stoned, thrice I suffered shipwreck, a night and a day I have been in the deep; In journeyings often, in perils of waters, in perils of robbers, in perils by mine own countrymen, in perils by the heathen, in perils in the city, in perils in the wilderness, in perils in the*

sea, in perils among false brethren; In weariness and painful-
ness, in watchings often, in hunger and thirst, in fastings
often, in cold and nakedness (2 Corinthians 11:24–27).

• *Ye know how through infirmity of the flesh I preached the*
gospel unto you at the first. And my temptation which was
in my flesh ye despised not, nor rejected . . . for I bear you
record, that, if it had been possible, ye would have plucked
out your own eyes, and have given them to me (Galatians
4:13–15).

Other examples of physical suffering include godly men such as
Epaphroditus (Philippians 2:25–30) and Timothy (1 Timothy 5:23).
Even Christ suffered physical weariness during His time of ministry
on this earth: "Jesus therefore, being wearied with his journey, sat
thus on the well: and it was about the sixth hour" (John 4:6).

As the writer says in Hebrews 11:32, time would fail us to tell
of all the others whose sufferings have been recorded in Scripture.
While some of those men and women certainly died as a result of
their afflictions—for instance, many of the prophets were tortured
to death—God was still faithful to them during their suffering.

All these examples were given for our benefit, so we might see
the necessity and surety of physical suffering, and might be comforted by God's care and sustenance through suffering. They were
given so we might rest in God's faithful character: as we read earlier,
what God was for Israel, He still is for us today.

Part IV

A Look at Our Response

Chapter 15

Scriptural Principles for Healing

WE HAVE LOOKED UPWARD AT our God to see who He is and what He has done, or has promised to do. We have looked outward at our circumstances, considering others who have suffered physically, and why we all must face affliction at some point. We can now turn our gaze inward, to reflect upon these truths and to consider a biblical response to physical suffering.

As we read in the previous section, there are many possible reasons we may suffer. However, the overarching focus of all suffering points toward God. He created us in order to have fellowship with us. Thus, everything He does in our lives is to help us know Him better and bring us into deeper intimacy with Himself.

While we certainly suffer afflictions stemming from purely physical causes, God has created our bodies and spirits to be so intricately conjoined that what affects us in one area affects us in another. For example, consider catching the flu. When all you can do is sleep on the sofa, when you can barely eat for lack of appetite or inability to keep anything down, it will most definitely affect your spiritual and mental capacities.

When your body feels miserable, your spirit will respond by feeling miserable with discouragement, despondency, or doubt. Since we are spiritual beings first and foremost—1 Corinthians 6:19 tells us our bodies are the *temples* of God, and James 2:26 states the "body without the spirit is dead"—we must focus on the spiritual before paying heed to the physical. Thus, when faced with physical suffering, our first response must be to go to God through prayer and His Word.

PRAYER

Consider your closest earthly friend, whether it be your spouse or some other person. If you were to only read *about* that friend, never talking together or listening in person, how well would you really know each other? It is the same in our relationship with God.

Prayer is a crucial part of truly knowing God, and a major theme throughout His Word. We are instructed to be in constant communication with our Heavenly Father, to literally "pray without ceasing" (1 Thessalonians 5:17). This is what prayer is: communication at its fullest. In fact, the original Hebrew and Greek offer many synonyms for *praying* which imply this fullness of communication—conversing, imploring, beseeching, worshiping earnestly, supplicating, petitioning, desiring greatly, entreating, pleading for mercy, interceding, groaning, or sighing.

Praying to God is not merely speaking words with our lips; it requires the involvement of our entire being. How can we possibly worship earnestly, plead for mercy, or pray with groaning and sighing unless our very heart and soul are involved? It is not simply a friendly chat, but a heart expression of total faith in the One who is sovereign over all. It is communion on the most intimate level.

Furthermore, we are commanded to pray. "Ask, and it shall be given you; seek, and ye shall find; knock, and it shall be opened unto you" (Matthew 7:7). Peter instructs us to cast our every concern and trouble before God (1 Peter 5:7), and Paul declares, "in every thing by prayer and supplication with thanksgiving let your requests be made known unto God" (Philippians 4:6). Those commands leave little room for doubt: we are to pray in every circumstance.

More specifically, as relates to our study, we are commanded to pray in times of suffering. In Psalm 50:15, the Lord instructs us to "call upon me in the day of trouble." Also, in the context of explaining Christ's role as our High Priest, Hebrews 4:16 directs us to "come boldly unto the throne of grace, that we may obtain mercy, and find grace to help in time of need." We see this practiced throughout the book of Nehemiah, as he responded to difficulty after difficulty by praying to God for help.

More precisely regarding prayer for physical well-being, 2 Kings 20 offers the account of Hezekiah, who begged God for healing. He was granted an extra fifteen years of life as a result of his prayer. Scripture also records John praying for his brother in Christ, Gaius, to enjoy good health (3 John 2).

Not only are prayers for physical health exemplified in God's Word, but even common sense suggests wherever there is lack or need, there is reason to pray. For instance, in times of war we pray for peace, and in times of drought we pray for rain. Thus, it follows that in times of sickness, we ought to pray for healing.

However, it is not enough just to utter words asking God to heal. Our prayers in general, and particularly our prayers for healing, must be made according to the standards set forth in His Word.

Although we are told to approach God's throne with boldness, we must also render proper humility and reverence. Old and New Testament accounts portray people kneeling as they prayed. Of course, physical posture does not determine heart attitude; however, these examples show the proper attitude of obeisance, the right heart posture to have when approaching a holy and righteous God. Even when we do not physically kneel during prayer, we ought to inwardly kneel before Him, bowing our hearts in humility before His throne.

Our prayers must also be made with thanksgiving. The book of Daniel gives many examples of Daniel praying in times of trouble, simultaneously offering supplication and thanksgiving to God. Philippians 4:6 and 1 Thessalonians 5:18 also instruct us to offer our prayers and requests *with* thanksgiving, not apart from it.

Additionally, we are to pray with persistence. Again, in the book of Daniel, we find him praying and entreating God until he received an answer. We also see this throughout Christ's earthly ministry, when those who were sick would beg Him for healing until He responded. Never were they condemned for repeating their requests. In fact, Christ likened our need for persistence to a man who begged his neighbor for bread until he got what he needed (Luke 11:5–13).

This persistence also implies passion and expectancy. That is, a vital heart interest in acquiring whatever is desired, and a firm belief in God's ability to fulfill that desire. James tells us the *fervent* prayer of a righteous man produces results, not requests made half-heartedly or with a double mind (James 5:16). He points to the example of Elijah, who prayed with passion and expectancy for both drought and rain—his fervent requests were granted.

Coupled with believing God will fulfill our requests, however, is the command to pray according to God's will. We see this principle established when Christ taught the disciples to pray, "Thy kingdom come. Thy will be done in earth as it is in heaven" (Matthew 6:10). We see it at the Mount of Olives when Christ prayed, "if it be possible, let this cup pass from me: nevertheless not as I will, but as thou wilt" (Matthew 26:39). We even read it in John's epistle, when he speaks of having confidence in God: "if we ask any thing according to his will, he heareth us: And if we know that he hear us, whatsoever we ask, we know that we have the petitions that we desired of him" (1 John 5:14–15).

Yet, although we must believe God will answer our requests in the way we desire, we also must acknowledge His ways and thoughts are far beyond our human comprehension. We must remember, even as we expect God to answer our prayers, He has promised to fulfill everything we truly *need*, not simply everything we desire. We must place our confidence in the God whom we studied at the beginning of this book—the One who has all knowledge, wisdom, and power; the One who loves us unconditionally; the One who is good and faithful.

The culmination of all these principles is found in the command to pray in Jesus' name. Again, as with the posture of kneeling, this is a heart attitude rather than a magic formula. We can only approach the throne of God under the banner of His Son—it is only through Christ's righteousness that the Father can look upon us and hear our prayers. Outside of His righteousness, we are covered in the blackness of sin.

However, "if I regard iniquity in my heart, the Lord will not hear me" (Psalm 66:18). Therefore, not only must we first experience redemptive cleansing by Jesus' blood, but we must also daily keep our hearts pure and righteous before Him. 1 John 1:9 reminds us to continually confess our sin, in order to be forgiven, cleansed, and able to regain fellowship with the Father. This fellowship, unbroken by sin, is also through the name of Jesus. This is the only way we can approach God the Father, through His Son Jesus Christ.

So, what happens when we follow these principles of prayer? When we adhere to every one of these standards, we have this promise from Christ: "Whatsoever ye shall ask in my name, that will I do, that the Father may be glorified in the Son. If ye shall ask any thing in my name, I will do it" (John 14:13–14).

Alternatively, when we refuse to pray about something, or fail to pray as God has instructed, we have a warning: "To him that knoweth to do good, and doeth it not, to him it is sin" (James 4:17). Failure to pray is sin, because it indicates a failure to believe God's Word and act upon it. It is sin because it demonstrates disobedience to God's commands.

Remember, prayer is an outward expression of the believer's inner faith and trust in His Savior. Thus, if we truly believe what God has said in His Word, then we *must* pray according to His standards and about all things.

FAITH

Not only do we need to pray about everything, but we also need to trust God will answer our prayers according to what glorifies Him most. We need to believe His plan for our lives is whatever He considers the absolute best for us—hence, our earlier study regarding the character and works of God. Most importantly, our faith must be placed in God alone—not in our good works, efforts, or prayers.

True faith is not merely wishing for something good or wanting something desperately. Rather, it carries the idea of heart-felt conviction and total confidence in the object of one's faith. As believers, this is characterized by genuine confidence in God and His Word (Proverbs 3:5–6), complete assurance of His leadership and sovereignty (Psalm 32:8), and total reliance upon His promises (Isaiah 26:3).[13]

This steadfast faith is commanded of every believer. Old and New Testament passages clearly state "the just shall live by faith." We also find explicit instructions regarding faith in Paul's first letter to Timothy, admonishing him to be "an example of the believers" in faith (1 Timothy 4:12), and to earnestly "follow after" faith (1 Timothy 6:11).

Additionally, Hebrews instructs us to approach God by faith: "But without faith it is impossible to please him: for he that cometh to God must believe that he is, and that he is a rewarder of them that diligently seek him" (Hebrews 11:6). In fact, the entire chapter surrounding this verse depicts those who had faith

---

13 Note: this exercising of faith differs from saving faith; one must already have repented of his sinfulness, and confessed a need for Christ's salvation, before he can seek God's blessing of healing.

in every word of God, and lived by faith no matter what, even to the point of dying for their faith in God. Those men and women were commended by God; He considered them righteous because of their faith, and was "not ashamed to be called their God" (Hebrews 11:16).

Clearly, if we are to have an ongoing relationship with our Creator and Savior, we must have faith that He is who He claims to be, and will do what He promises to do. We must have total confidence in God and His words, throughout every circumstance of our lives here on earth.

We are also commanded to manifest our faith by our works. In other words, our visible expressions of righteous living will testify of our inner faith in God's Word. For instance, the men and women of Hebrews 11 did not merely profess faith in God, but actually proved their faith by their actions, living and even dying for their beliefs. Only those who whole-heartedly believe something will sacrifice their very lives for it!

This principle is further explained in the book of James. In chapter 2, the man who merely professes faith is contrasted with one who truly lives out his faith, by an illustration of helping someone in need:

> If a brother or sister be naked, and destitute of daily food, And one of you say unto them, Depart in peace, be ye warmed and filled; notwithstanding ye give them not those things which are needful to the body; what doth it profit? Even so faith, if it hath not works, is dead, being alone (James 2:15–17).

James goes on to compare this person, who professes faith but does not act on it, to the devils who acknowledge God and tremble. Their "faith" is certainly not a saving faith, and the man who fails to show his faith by his actions is no better off than they are!

James also offers the example of Abraham. By offering his beloved son Isaac upon the altar, signifying his obvious intention to obey God completely, he was counted as righteous. Notice, James does *not* say Abraham was considered righteous for simply acknowledging God's saving power—as the demons do. Rather, he was called righteous because his particular actions demonstrated his faith to all around him.

The harlot, Rahab, is also given as an example of true faith. She believed God would destroy her city and deliver it to Israel. When two Israelites came to spy out the land, she hid them from the authorities and later helped them escape. In return, her life was spared when her city was destroyed. She, a harlot and a pagan Gentile, was considered righteous in God's eyes because of the visible manifestation of her faith.

James concludes this section with one final comparison, to further establish the imperativeness of showing our faith by our works: "For as the body without the spirit is dead, so faith without works is dead also" (James 2:26). Could it be said any more simply?

JAMES 5:13-16

Consistent personal prayer and continued faith in God are the main criterion established in Scripture for seeking physical healing. We should also consider James 5:13–16, a passage which directly mentions the issue of seeking healing:

Is any among you afflicted? let him pray. Is any merry? let him sing psalms. Is any sick among you? let him call for the elders of the church; and let them pray over him, anointing him with oil in the name of the Lord: And the prayer of faith shall save the sick, and the Lord shall raise him up; and if he have committed sins, they shall be forgiven him. Confess your faults one to another, and pray one for another, that ye may be healed. The effectual fervent prayer of a righteous man availeth much.

Although many people view this passage as a guideline for dealing with prolonged illness, the emphasis is actually on prayer, rather than sickness. James begins by exhorting believers to pray when afflicted, and sing praise when merry. He then encourages the "prayer of faith" for those who are sick. We will look at this prayer in a moment, but first let us define the intended audience for this exhortation.

The word that is translated *sick* comes from the Greek word *astheneo*, which means to be feeble, diseased, sick, or weak. Although it can be used in a spiritual manner, it is typically used in the physical sense to describe those near death, command believers to visit and care for the sick, or in the case of Christ, to heal multitudes who suffered lameness, blindness, or other physical maladies.

In this particular passage, the simplest and most literal interpretation of the word *sick* also refers to the physical realm. Nothing in the surrounding context contradicts that.[14]

Additionally, we know the body and spirit are interconnected—what affects one will affect the other. Serious or chronic physical

14 Refer also to the principles of biblical hermeneutics listed within chapter 9, "Work of Atonement."

afflictions are thus systemic in every sense of the word. As the body collapses, so does the spirit. As the flesh weakens, so does the mind. Concentration is difficult. Articulation is next to impossible.

Therefore, we can reasonably interpret this passage as being directed to those who were not only physically sick but emotionally despondent, unable to pray and losing faith in God.

After all, can the despondent one pray passionately? Can the doubting one pray expectantly? Consider how one commentator explains this:

> . . . *when the body may be racked with pain and the mind considerably disturbed, it is not easy for the sufferer unaided to turn his thoughts in any articulated or concentrated manner to prayer, and he needs the consolation of other Christians in what may be for him a period of much spiritual distress.*[15]

Those who are suffering to the point of such spiritual distress are to call for their church elders, who can come alongside and intercede on their behalf.[16] For the one who is seriously ill, even the mere sight and sound of this gathering would be a spiritual balm.

By being together in the same location, the elders are able to pray more specifically and passionately on the afflicted one's behalf, articulating both physical and spiritual needs. Consider this for a moment: How can our church leaders pray specifically

---

15   R.V.G. Tasker, *The General Epistle of James: An Introduction and Commentary* (Grand Rapids: Wm. B. Eerdmans Publishing Company, 1983), 129.

16   Elders were established in the early church to care for the spiritual needs within their local body of believers. They are commanded to watch over and give account for each individual under their leadership (Hebrews 13:17).

for us without any personal interaction? How can they pray passionately without coming face-to-face with our afflictions?

This time of focused prayer together also provides a powerful reminder of prayer's effectiveness. As supplications are answered and the afflicted is strengthened spiritually, if not also physically, everyone involved will confirm what James states at the end of this passage: the "fervent prayer of a righteous man availeth much."

In addition to praying for the sick one, the elders are also to anoint him or her with oil. Anointing simply refers to rubbing or smearing a substance on someone's skin; in those days, olive oil was typically used, sometimes with a mixture of medicines and herbs.

This action was often symbolic. In the Old Testament, anointing a man with oil signified setting him apart for God—for instance, when David was anointed as Israel's future king, he was publicly set apart for God's purposes. It was also a medicinal practice—in the New Testament, the good Samaritan anointed and cared for an injured traveler (Luke 10:34) and the apostles anointed those who were sick (Mark 6:13).

Contrary to the Roman Catholic sacrament of last rites, this act of anointing with oil is not sacred or mystical in itself. Rather, it is merely a practical application of medicine, an outward sign of an inward reliance upon God. Recalling the previous section on faith, it is a visible work demonstrating the inward belief of the sick one and the elders.

Additionally, the act of anointing was usually coupled with praying. James instructs the elders to anoint the sick one in "the name of the Lord." The use of His name must characterize not only the anointing, but also the praying, as we saw in the section on prayer. This serves as a reminder of God's unique power and sovereignty. He alone has power to heal; men's words or medicines can do nothing on their own.

Peter attested to this truth in Acts 3, when he and John were given power to heal a lame man. They commanded him to rise up and walk "in the name of Jesus Christ of Nazareth" (Acts 3:6). When bystanders wondered at the miracle, Peter responded, "Ye men of Israel, why marvel ye at this . . . as though by our own power or holiness we had made this man to walk?" (Acts 3:12). Healing was brought about by Christ's name alone. Peter and John were merely instruments of His power and authority over illness.

Once the elders anoint and pray over the sick one, James says "the prayer of faith shall save the sick." This returns us to the main point of the passage, which is to pray.

Since man is primarily a spiritual being, his spiritual needs must take priority over his physical needs. In this case, if the afflicted one is an unbeliever, the elders should pray for salvation. If the person is living with unconfessed sin, the elders should pray for repentance and restoration to God. The result of their prayer is also spiritual: the sick one will be saved. According to the original Greek, this refers to salvation from sin, rather than physical deliverance from illness.

In addition to spiritual deliverance, James also promises "the Lord shall raise him up." This most likely refers to further spiritual healing, whereby the afflicted one's spirit is bolstered and encouraged enough to regain faith in God's providence. It could possibly also involve physical healing, either immediately or in the future. However, the major focus here is on spiritual health rather than physical.

The point of James 5:13–16 is not how to procure immediate physical healing, but how to restore the spiritual health of one who is sick. It is not about finding physical relief from suffering, but how suffering will lead us to find God and be drawn closer to Him.

This priority of spiritual well–being should characterize our response to physical suffering, and be reflected in our prayers and continued faith in God.

Chapter 16

Physical Means of Healing

IN ADDITION TO THE SPIRITUAL principles given in His Word, God has also provided physical aids we can use to seek healing. Doctors and medicines can often help us determine the physical cause of our suffering, remedy various problems, and help alleviate some of the symptoms.

As long as we seek our Creator's help first, we can certainly take advantage of whatever else He has provided through His marvelous creation. Even when we cannot discern the spiritual purpose for our illness, these medical means can often help us find a physical cause for whatever we are suffering.

During His earthly ministry, Christ spoke of mankind's need for physicians (Matthew 9:12). Our benevolent Father has provided us with those physicians, and given them necessary skills to help us. He expects us to take advantage of their wisdom, knowledge, and ability. In fact, their expertise provides a very practical means of physical improvement.

Also, we see examples throughout all four Gospels of men and women who visited doctors in search of healing (*see* Mark 5:26). They were not condemned for such a practice. Even Luke, the author of one of the Gospels and the book of Acts, was a doctor— Paul called him the "beloved physician" (Colossians 4:14). Surely, if doctors were not to be sought after, these examples would not have been included in our New Testament.

We have also been given the gift of medicine. Consider the creation of herbs and fruits in the first chapter of Genesis. These plants are used not only for daily nourishment, but also for their medicinal properties. God called His creation of these things *good*, essentially advocating our use of them (Genesis 1:11–12). He also includes examples throughout His Word of using medicine to attain healing.

In 2 Kings 20, the first verse says King Hezekiah was "sick unto death" due to a malignant disease. When he begged God for healing, he not only recovered from his illness, but even gained fifteen additional years of life. God chose to heal him through the use of medicine: "And Isaiah said, Take a lump of figs. And they took and laid it on the boil, and he recovered" (2 Kings 20:7).

Moving to the Gospels, Luke 10 shares the parable of the good Samaritan. As he was traveling one day, he discovered a man who had been beaten, stripped, and left for dead by the side of the road. Although the main point of this parable was how to love our neighbors (Luke 10:27), Christ also advocated the use of medicine for physical ailments. As we know, the Samaritan traveler chose to care for the wounded man. "He had compassion on him, and went to him, and bound up his wounds, pouring in oil and wine . . ." (Luke 10:33–34). Oil eased the pain and wine cleansed the wound. If we were not to use such aids available to us, surely He would not have included their use within His parable.

Continuing on to the epistles, we read Paul's instruction for Timothy to "use a little wine for thy stomach's sake and thine often infirmities" (1 Timothy 5:23). Once again, we find encouragement for the use of medicine as a remedy for physical ailments.

Finally, the book of Revelation suggests medicine is useful even in the New Jerusalem, the final dwelling place of all the saints. John's heavenly vision describes the Holy City, including the tree of life "which bare twelve manner of fruits, and yielded her fruit every month: and the leaves of the tree were for the healing of the nations" (Revelation 22:1–2; Ezekiel 47:12).

In addition to these examples, Scripture also provides us with some guidelines for seeking medical care. More specifically, it warns us against tempting and rejecting God in our search for healing.

First, refusing to use doctors and medicine may selfishly challenge God. Consider Luke's account of Christ's temptation in the wilderness. Each time Satan proposed a temptation, Christ responded with Scripture. His final response was a command: "It is said, Thou shalt not tempt the Lord thy God" (Luke 4:12, *from* Deuteronomy 6:16).

So, how does this apply to the rejection of medicinal help in time of illness?

As one theologian explains: "to expose myself to any danger naturally destructive, with the vain presumption that God will protect and defend me from the ruinous consequences of my imprudent conduct, is *to tempt God*."[17] The notes in the Geneva Bible further

---

17   Adam Clarke, *The New Testament of Our Lord and Saviour Jesus Christ* (Nashville: Abingdon-Cokesbury Press, 1831), volume 1, note on Matthew 4:7.

illustrate the action of tempting God as "doubting his power, refusing lawful means, and abusing his graces."[18]

In other words, rejecting the help God has provided for us is foolish and sinful. He has given us common sense and He expects us to use it. He has provided us with various forms of medical care, expecting us to seek it out in times of physical need. To do otherwise is to reject His gifts, doubt His goodness and provision, and unnecessarily challenge His character and His Word.

Second, God's help must be sought alongside medical care. Scripture is very clear: we are not condemned for either suffering physically or using available medical help. However, neglecting to seek God's divine care during those times is a blatant rejection of Him.

We find this illustrated in 2 Chronicles 16, when King Asa was suffering from a condition similar to gout. It began in his feet and traveled throughout his body, intensifying and worsening. Yet, he chose to seek only the help of his physicians. "His disease was exceeding great: yet in his disease he sought not to the LORD, but to the physicians. And Asa slept with his fathers, and died in the one and fortieth year of his reign" (2 Chronicles 16:12–13).

King Asa's decision to seek medical care is not censured. Rather, it was the manner in which he sought the care—refusing to seek God's help before and alongside the physician's abilities. The consequence of this refusal was "Asa slept with his fathers, and died." His sole focus upon the human ability of his physicians, and his neglect and rejection of the divine ability of his Creator, led to his death.

---

18   *The Geneva Bible: a Facsimile of the 1599 Edition with Undated Sternhold & Hopkins Psalms* (Ozark, Missouri: L.L. Brown Publishing, 1990), Deuteronomy 6:16.

Of course, fulfilling a set of criterion does not automatically guarantee physical healing. Praying, exercising faith, seeking doctors, and using medicine do not compose a magic formula to make illness disappear. Yes, we should do all these things—but we must always remember healing takes place on God's terms, not ours.

Sometimes He may even choose to deliver us *through* the affliction rather than out of it. Remember Paul? He prayed several times for God to remove his thorn in the flesh. He certainly had faith in God's power to heal, and he likely also sought medicinal help. Yet, God chose to withhold immediate physical healing, promising instead divine help to live with his affliction:

> *And he said unto me, My grace is sufficient for thee: for my strength is made perfect in weakness. Most gladly therefore will I rather glory in my infirmities, that the power of Christ may rest upon me* (2 Corinthians 12:9).

Chapter 17

Sinful Attempts at Healing

SO, WHEN SUFFERING PHYSICALLY, WE are to seek God's help first and medical help second. Are these the only avenues of healing available to us? What about faith healers, who claim the power to heal physical afflictions?

Men such as Oral Roberts, Kenneth Copeland, and Benny Hinn are famous for their miracle services, where they appear to heal hundreds of people. Any one of them may call out an audience member who is suffering from some sort of affliction. Someone lays hands on the person, and words or prayers are said. The afflicted one might fall down, become weak, or suddenly stand upright, depending on the manner of healing performed. Is that person truly healed?

Take a moment to consider the roots of faith healing. Think about witch doctors' fetishes and occultist black magic. Consider Christian Scientists, psychic healers, and performers of so-called bloodless surgeries. Note even the Roman Catholic Church, which has promised healing through ancient bones and relics.

Multitudes of people with disease-riddled bodies have flocked to these religions over the years, grasping any promise of help in their search for healing. Yet, do these alternatives actually heal? More importantly, as children of God, are we to seek their help?

After all, they preach the power of having faith, which we already believe is imperative for the Christian. They pray, they claim ability from the Holy Spirit, and people actually seem to be healed by their power. Men rise up from their wheelchairs. Women can suddenly read without glasses. Crooked arms are straightened. Blood sugar levels return to normal. Depression disappears.

So, what should a discerning believer—who seeks to respond biblically—notice about these promises of healing?

First, a common thread in all of these healings is the need for faith. However, faith is always placed in something other than God. Sick people are told to trust in the power of human hands or minds, or a piece of wood or bone, rather than in the Creator and Sustainer of life.

Second, these healings are always done according to the desires of the faith healers—in their tents or auditoriums, according to their schedules, and in their own ways. Their healings are never according to "God's will be done." If they proclaim someone healed, the person *better* be healed! If the person is not healed, then he or she must not have had enough faith to be healed. Failure is blamed on everyone *but* the faith healer.

Third, many conditions seemingly healed are actually rather subjective. It is important for us to recognize three main types of diseases: *psychogenic* (of the mind), *functional* (soreness or weakness), and *organic* (withered or missing limbs, etc.). Closer study reveals most faith healers heal only psychogenic and functional conditions, which can be easily faked or imagined and are not objectively measureable. Furthermore, these supposed healings are manifest through subjective measures such as hypnosis, power of suggestion, and positive thinking—which involve only the realm of emotions, and easily dominate those weakened by illness.

Finally, and perhaps the most dangerous part of these healings, faith healers claim to heal unseen problems such as cancers or diabetes. Their transient cures often cause sick individuals to refuse necessary medications or treatments, causing them to actually grow worse instead of better. Any who claim to have been healed of such organic diseases either find the illness returning later—if it ever left—or have actually improved with the help of medical care.

Why then do multitudes of men and women flock to these alternative healings? Remember what we saw in James 5: those who are weakened physically are usually also weakened mentally and spiritually, making them more vulnerable to Satan's whisper of temptation to seek anything but God for deliverance.

Satan's constant goal is to make us doubt God: "Skin for skin, yea, all that a man hath will he give for his life. But put forth thine hand now, and touch his bone and his flesh, and he will curse thee to thy face" (Job 2:3–4). Once we have given in to doubt, refusing to trust our Lord, it is easy to seek an emotional high. It is easy for a person weakened in body and spirit to be bolstered by the claim of miracles, confusing an emotional thrill for a strengthening of faith. However, good health does not bring ultimate satisfaction. Just as all the money in the world cannot make a man truly happy, neither can a body free from disease.

Compare the acts of these faith healers with the healings of Christ and His apostles. In New Testament times, medical science was extremely limited. There were countless more incurable diseases and plagues than there are today. Yet, Christ healed multitudes who flocked to Him. He healed the woman who merely touched the hem of His garment. He healed the child whose father came begging for help.

He healed through a simple word or single touch. He healed instantaneously and completely; there was no progressive healing of natural processes or recuperation periods. He healed everyone as they came to Him; there was no scheduled service at a designated tent or auditorium. He healed all kinds of diseases, even organic diseases, such as a man with a withered hand, another one sick with palsy, and a paralytic. He even raised the dead—and no faith healer can raise someone who has been in the grave for three days, as Christ did with Lazarus.

All these differences abound; yet, they do not touch the main distinction between Christ's healings and those of charismatics. In Christ's time, the Scriptures were not yet completed and the gospel was new to man. So Christ healed, not to keep people healthy, but to authenticate the gospel and prove His divine authority over all things.

Consider the paralytic man who was lowered through a roof by his four friends. Christ healed him so everyone would know "the Son of man hath power on earth to forgive sins" (Matthew 9:6). Yet those who claim to heal today do so merely to keep people healthy and happy. They have no interest in spreading the gospel. They have no need to prove the authority of Scripture.

Christ was not the only one who healed; He also gave power to the apostles and certain other disciples (Acts 8:6–7). Each of their healings coincided with the initial proclamation of the gospel, and served to authenticate its truth, to confirm God's revelation to man through Jesus Christ. Not so today, when Scripture has been complete for almost two thousand years and we have the Holy Spirit to open our spiritual eyes. We no longer need signs to prove the veracity of Christ's message, the gospel of redemption.

Those who genuinely healed in New Testament times used their gift of healing to help establish and grow the church, not to increase their own programs or agendas. They were not trying to make a name for themselves or draw bigger crowds. They did not perform miracles just for the sake of performing miracles. Rather, they had a higher purpose of glorifying God's name and exalting His truth. Healing was a credential to their ministry, not their central focus.

On the other hand, faith healers today are men and women without discernment who seek their own glory. Their healings are similar to those at the church of Corinth, where authentic spiritual gifts were frequently counterfeited. They twist the words of Scripture to fit their purposes and lay hands hastily, without seeking God's will through fervent prayer, as Paul instructed Timothy (1 Timothy 5:22). They operate with sinful methods, under satanic delusions, and produce faulty reports.

These men and women deceive millions of people every day, causing great spiritual harm. Those who seek the thrills promised by faith healers often find dissatisfaction with Christ as a result, for they are seeking to be fed by miracles rather than by Christ. They begin to believe willpower is the basis for faith and life, rather than the grace and strength of God. However, they are deceived. Their thinking is skewed by false doctrine.

Faith healers claim it is God's will for every sick person to be healed. Yet they cannot heal themselves, as is documented by their illnesses and deaths throughout the years. If total healing was God's will, would they have even suffered in the first place?

Their teaching is false. God does not remove our sin nature at the point of salvation; why would He remove the consequences of that sin nature? If He does not remove sin from His permissive will for believers, why would He remove sickness, a direct result of sin's presence in the world? If it *was* removed, Christianity would turn into a mere panacea for physical illness, a magic formula for people seeking healthy bodies. Repentance would be irrelevant, and faith in God would become unnecessary.

Faith healers also seek to turn the miraculous into the ordinary. However, by definition, a miracle is any occurrence which is *out of* the ordinary.

In Wayne Grudem's *Systematic Theology*, miracles are defined as a "less common kind of God's activity in which he arouses people's awe and wonder and bears witness to himself."[19] Notice the words "less common." Miracles do not happen frequently, and are not accomplished by use of natural means, such as medicine or the process of time. They occur only occasionally, always when natural means are wholly impossible.

A miraculous healing would be the woman on her deathbed, with no possible hope of recuperation, who suddenly has no trace of the cancer that once ravaged her body. It would be the man who has suffered lifelong blindness, who suddenly regains his sight without the help of doctors, medicines, or treatments.

Yes, our God is still the God of miracles. He is still the same

---

19   Wayne Grudem, *Systematic Theology* (Grand Rapids: Zondervan Publishing House, 2000), 355.

God who parted the Red Sea, protected Daniel in the lions' den, and called Lazarus forth from the grave. But miracles, by definition, are rare! They do not happen at seven o'clock every Saturday night in Manhattan, or every Sunday morning at eleven o'clock in Los Angeles. They happen according to God's timing and will alone.

When people find themselves healed today, while it may feel like a miracle to one who has suffered so intently for so long, it generally can be explained by God's working through natural means to heal them. The healing is still of God, when it comes, but it is not usually an actual miracle. True healing occurs on God's terms alone: according to His perfect will and timing. It is never solely by the hands or words of a man.

Faith healers today may believe they are actually healing men and women, or they may simply be deceiving the masses. Either way, their healings oppose biblical truth; they conflict with the laws of God and nature. Faith healers should not be sought by those who trust in God.

Part V

A Look at God's Response

Chapter 18

Putting It All Together

SO, NOW WHAT? IF WE believe all we have studied about God, if
we obey Scripture's commands to pray about everything and trust
God completely, and if we reject sinful attempts to find satisfaction
outside of God—what then? What are we supposed to do with all
of this information? Let us review what we have studied so far, to
see how it all fits together.

We looked first at the character and names of God, and saw He
is absolutely unchanging. He sees and knows all ('El Ro'i), and is
utterly wise in using all knowledge for our benefit. He is wholly
good. He loves us unconditionally and eternally.

He is altogether sovereign ('El Shaddai, 'El 'Elyon). He directs
and provides for us each day—not for us only, but even for His
entire creation (Jehovah–jireh). He is the God we can call upon in
any circumstance. His character is reflected in His names, and His
names establish His reputation. His character and reputation are
wholly unchanging.

We then considered how His character has been shown
throughout history: from creation, to the leading of Israel, to the
earthly ministry of Christ. We saw how He led and cared for His

people, both Jews and Gentiles, and how He healed spiritually and physically.

Beyond this, we studied Christ's work on the cross, where He forever settled the debt of our sin. He suffered as the only perfect Lamb, the only acceptable sacrifice for our transgressions against a holy God. In doing so, He provided a way for us to be made whole again and regain full intimacy with God.

We discovered Christ's sacrifice on the cross did not negate sin's presence in the world, or remove sin's consequences, such as sickness and death. However, we found hope in the promise of future glorification. Someday our souls and bodies will be completely transformed from a state of humiliation and mortality to a state of eternal glory, as we dwell wholly complete in the presence of God the Father—free from sin and sin's consequences.

After considering God's character and works, we looked at our circumstances: Why do we suffer affliction? Is it truly God's will for us? We saw God's wisdom and sovereignty not only *allow* suffering, but even *promise* it. However, He also promises good things from our suffering: we will know Him more intimately, glorify Him more fully, and become testimonies of His goodness and faithfulness to all generations.

We also recognized the examples of great men of God, even Christ Himself, suffering illness or weariness in the flesh. Thus, we determined it is truly within God's perfect plan for His children to face physical suffering.

Finally, after looking at God and our circumstances, we considered how to respond in a manner obedient to Scripture and glorifying to God. We saw the spiritual principles of earnestly praying according to biblical guidelines, and having genuine faith in God and His promises, believing God is who He claims and will do what He promises. We also saw the benefit of using medical resources God has provided for us.

Next, we considered faith healings, noting the general weakness and emotional vulnerability of those who seek such healings. We also considered the definition of *miracles*, which are not performed regularly, on command, or by natural means; they are rare and only by the hand of God. We concluded such faith healings are faulty, self-centered, and even sinful.

So, now what? Do we expect God to heal because of His goodness? Do we expect Him to *not* heal because He has promised affliction? How should we wait for His response to our prayers, faith in Him, and obedience to His commands?

Chapter 19

Waiting for Healing

AS WE SEEK DIVINE HELP in our suffering, there are a handful of pertinent commands given to us within God's Word, which we must obey.[20]

First, we must keep our hearts pure before God. None of us will be perfect until eternity; therefore, continual confession of sin is necessary for our prayers to be heard. The psalmist declares in Psalm 66:18, "If I regard iniquity in my heart, the Lord will not hear me." God cannot abide the presence of sin, and He turns His face away from those who continually dwell in sin. Fellowship is broken, and communication is rendered ineffective.

We are responsible to seek His forgiveness and cleansing when we commit sin. Only then can fellowship can be restored. "If we confess our sins, he is faithful and just to forgive us our sins, and to cleanse us from all unrighteousness" (1 John 1:9). Then, and only then, will He hear our supplications and pleas for help during times of trouble. Our daily prayer ought to be the same as David's in Psalm 51:1–3.

---

20   For further suggestions regarding waiting for healing *see* Appendix C: "Practical Suggestions for Dealing with Illness."

Have mercy upon me, O God, according to thy lovingkindness: according unto the multitude of thy tender mercies blot out my transgressions. Wash me throughly from mine iniquity, and cleanse me from my sin. For I acknowledge my transgressions: and my sin is ever before me.

Second, we must be surrendered to God's will. He is our Master Potter, and we are merely clay in His hands. He determines what shape we will take. As we surrender to Him, He will fashion us into the shape which best accomplishes His purposes, not merely whatever shape is easiest for us to live. He chooses to remove our afflictions only when it will most glorify His name and proclaim His deity, not according to our sense of comfort.

Third, we must patiently rest in Him. The first chapter of James reminds us trials produce patience, or steadfast endurance, and endurance brings forth completeness in Christ. James 5 reminds us of the prophets and Job, who experienced God's goodness and mercy as they remained patient through suffering. The psalmist also exhorts us to rest steadfastly in God: "wait on the LORD: be of good courage, and he shall strengthen thine heart: wait, I say, on the LORD" (Psalm 27:14).

Fourth, we are to remain steadfast in thanksgiving, even while we wait expectantly for His healing touch. "Rejoice evermore. Pray without ceasing. In every thing give thanks: for this is the will of God in Christ Jesus concerning you" (1 Thessalonians 5:16–18). We can do all these things because He is faithful, and will not tempt or try us beyond what we can handle (1 Corinthians 10:13). Whether He provides healing or allows continued suffering, He will never lead us to a situation which we cannot survive by His grace.

Fifth, we must continue faithfully in prayer. God does not always heal instantly: consider the account of Eutychus, who fell out of a third-story window and was presumed dead (Acts 20). Paul prayed over Eutychus, and promised the crowd he was still alive, then ate and continued on his way. Eutychus still suffered the effects of his fall. His healing, though promised, was not immediate. It came about through the process of time and natural means.

So often, we assume God always heals instantly. When He does not, we stop praying. We get tired of repeatedly asking for the same thing, or we see some progress in our health, and stop praying for healing. We get busy with life and other concerns, and stop praying for healing.

However, we are to pray persistently until we perceive God's answer. For instance, after Paul prayed several times about his thorn in the flesh, he received a definite answer to *stop* seeking healing: "For this thing I besought the Lord thrice, that it might depart from me. And he said unto me, My grace is sufficient for thee: for my strength is made perfect in weakness" (1 Corinthians 12:8–9). God clearly indicated his infirmity would not be healed! To continue praying for healing beyond that point would have showed unbelief in God's answer, and a lack of trust in His grace. It would have been sinful.

We must also pray persistently for other believers. We are to intercede for them, bear their burdens before the throne of God, and "pray one for another that ye may be healed" (James 5:16). This particular type of intercession is exemplified throughout the New Testament.

Many men and women were healed from sickness as the apostles interceded for them. Peter was delivered from prison because "prayer was made without ceasing of the church unto God for him" (Acts 12:5). John even records a prayer for his brother Gaius to "prosper and be in health" (3 John 2). We, too, are to pray for the spiritual and physical well-being of our brothers and sisters in Christ.

Sixth, we must exhort one another to remain steadfast in faith and sound doctrine. Remember the false views of the atonement, the sinful assumption that believers are not supposed to be sick, and the deceitful practices of faith healers? We are to steadfastly reject those lies.

As we continue in this sinful world, where man ever attempts his own path to God, we are certain to discover even more false teachings and sinful practices. "In the latter times some shall depart from the faith, giving heed to seducing spirits, and doctrines of devils" (1 Timothy 4:1). John also declared, "even now are there many antichrists" (1 John 2:18).

We must constantly be on guard to discern truth from error, and refute whatever (or whoever) contradicts God's Word, as 1 John 4:1–6 exhorts us:

> *Beloved, believe not every spirit, but try the spirits whether they are of God: because many false prophets are gone out into the world. Hereby know ye the Spirit of God: Every spirit that confesseth that Jesus Christ is come in the flesh is of God: And every spirit that confesseth not that Jesus Christ is come in the flesh is not of God: and this is that spirit of antichrist, whereof ye have heard that it should come; and even now already is it in the world*

. . . They are of the world: therefore speak they of the world, and the world heareth them. We are of God: he that knoweth God heareth us; he that is not of God heareth not us. Hereby know we the spirit of truth, and the spirit of error.

Chapter 20

Lack of Healing

WHAT IF GOD CHOOSES NOT to heal? We may seek God's help first and medicinal help second. We may be persistent and passionate in our prayers. We may remain strong in belief, sound in doctrine, and steadfast in faith. Yet, all this does not guarantee healing. All this does not determine whether God will remove our afflictions.

When He *does* choose to heal, the healing is merely temporary—death has passed upon all of us, because we are all sinners (Romans 5:12). Yet, sometimes He chooses not to heal. We cannot determine His choice. Therefore, even as we obey biblical principles, we must also be willing to continue suffering.

Once again, Scripture provides examples. Godly men and women remained seriously ill because it glorified God. Trophimus was left in sickness at Miletum (2 Timothy 4:20); we never read whether he recovered. Epaphroditus suffered sickness "nigh unto death" for the sake of spreading the gospel (Philippians 2:25–27). Although many prayed for his recovery, and God did eventually heal him, he remained deathly ill for a while. Paul also suffered a serious affliction, a thorn in his flesh, which God chose not to heal.

Our examples are not limited to Scripture. Think of Fanny Crosby, the great hymn-writer who suffered blindness. If she had lived being able to see, would she have penned all those faith-filled hymns of praise to God? Think about Joni Eareckson, who suffered a childhood accident and remains a paraplegic to this day. She has a ministry to others who are disabled which she may never have experienced otherwise.

Not to compare my influence and effectiveness with theirs, but I have also experienced opportunities to minister, which would not have existed if God had spared me from sickness or healed me in the hospital. This book would not have been written. Other ministries of encouragement and exhortation would simply never have existed.

There have also been great advancements in other areas of life by those God chose not to heal. For instance, Lieutenant Matthew Maury suffered a severe leg injury which ended not only his assignment at sea, but also his naval career. However, he went on to study the records of past ships and contributed significantly to the charting of winds and ocean currents.[21] Other great men and women have made significant contributions to cultural and scientific fields, as a result of being limited physically by illness or injury.

Time and space limit the stories we could share. Yet, our stories would all prove the same truth: when God chooses not to heal, it is because we can glorify Him better through our suffering than through our wholeness. Sometimes, that glory may even be through death.

---

21   Andrew W. Blackwood, Jr., *The Holy Spirit in Your Life* (Grand Rapids: Baker Book House, 1957), 120–122.

Death is not something we anticipate for anyone, even though eternity will far surpass our earthly lives. Yet, death is a natural progression of life. As soon as we are born, we begin to die: "a time to be born, and a time to die; a time to plant, and a time to pluck up that which is planted" (Ecclesiastes 3:2). Life is a vapor which exists for a moment, then vanishes completely.

However, God sovereignly controls the length of each life. Man's "days are determined, the number of his months are with thee, thou hast appointed his bounds that he cannot pass" (Job 14:5). God ordained the number of our days before we were even conceived. We can neither lengthen nor shorten them on our own.

Sometimes, God ordains our days to be concluded by terrible illness. Sometimes, He lovingly takes His child home by severe physical suffering. It is certainly not easy to watch a loved one suffer toward death; however, He alone determines the span of every life.

For those who know God as their Savior, death is not a thing to be mourned. It is a home-going. Death is merely the soul's passing from a sin-filled world to a perfect eternal home, from a broken state to a glorified state.

Yes, it is hard for those left behind. It leaves a gaping hole. It hurts. Yet, God gently comforts us: "Precious in the sight of the LORD is the death of his saints" (Psalm 116:15). He does not willingly grieve or afflict us; He has "compassion according to multitude of his mercies" (Lamentations 3:32–33). God does not delight in ordaining death for His children. If we truly believe this, death will not leave us sorrowful for long.

Sometimes it requires stronger faith to trust God when healing does not come. It is a harder path, but He still leads. It is more physically difficult, but the spiritual rewards can be bountiful. Although we might suffer tremendously here on earth, we look forward to an eternity of abundant, glorious life with Him! He promises to provide good from our suffering: beauty from ashes and joy out of mourning (Isaiah 61:3).

When healing does not come, we must still remain steadfast in faith and doctrine. We must continue in prayer for ourselves and others, as He commands. We must learn to live rejoicing evermore, giving thanks in everything. Whether we are healthy or sick, comfortable or afflicted, full of life or knocking at death's door—this is His will for each one of us.

Let us remember these truths, and give ourselves wholly to them, that our profiting my appear to all (1 Timothy 4:15).

God's promise is not freedom from trials in the race;
But power to transcend them through His sufficing grace.

Not rest instead of labor, but in the labor rest;
Not calm instead of tempest, but calm when sore depressed.

Not light instead of darkness, not joy instead of grief;
But brightness in the midnight, and in the woe relief.

Not gain instead of losses, not ease instead of pain;
But balm upon the anguish, and losses bringing gain.

Not strength instead of weakness, no smile instead of tears;
Not peace instead of conflict, not song instead of tears.

But weakness filled with power, and tears with radiance spread,
And peace amid the battle, and song e'er fears are fled.[22]

---

22   Norman Douty, "In All These Things."

Thine, O Lord, is the greatness,
and the power, and the glory, and the victory, and the majesty:
for all that is in the heaven and in the earth is thine:
thine is the kingdom, O Lord, and thou art exalted as head above all.
    But riches and honor come from thee, and thou reignest over all;
and in thine hand is power and might;
and in thine hand it is to make great, and give strength unto all.

—1 Chronicles 29:11–12

Appendix A

Healings Performed during Christ's Earthly Ministry

Healing	Matthew	Mark	Luke	John
Nobleman's son				4:46–54
Demon-possessed man		1:23–28	4:33–36	
Peter's mother-in-law	8:14–15	1:29–31	4:38–39	
Multitudes	4:23–25	1:34, 39	4:42–44	
Man with leprosy	8:2–4	1:40–45	5:12–14	
Paralytic man	9:2–8	2:3–12	5:18–26	
Lame Man				5:1–9
Man with withered hand	12:9–13	3:1–5	6:6–10	
Centurion's servant	8:5–13		7:1–10	
Widow's son			7:11–15	

Healing	Matthew	Mark	Luke	John
Blind and mute demon-possessed man	12:22–23		11:14–26	
Demon-possessed men	8:28–34	5:1–20	8:26–39	
Jairus' daughter	9:18–26	5:22–43	8:41–56	
Woman with issue of blood	9:20–22	5:25–34	8:43–48	
Blind men	9:27–31			
Mute demon-possessed man	9:32–33			
Multitudes	9:35–38			
Multitudes	14:34–36	6:53–56		
Syrophenician's daughter	15:21–28	7:24–30		
Deaf-mute man		7:31–37		
Blind man		8:22–25		
Demon-possessed boy	17:14–18	9:14–29	9:38–42	
Blind man				9:1–7
Lazarus				11:1–44
Crippled woman			13:10–17	
Man with dropsy			14:2–4	
Ten lepers			17:12–19	
Blind men	20:29–34	10:46–52	18:35–43	
Man's ear			22:49–51	

Appendix B

General Purposes of Trials

FIRST OF ALL, WE SUFFER trials for the purpose of revealing God.

- Trials reveal the works of God:

  And as Jesus passed by, he saw a man which was blind from his birth.
  And his disciples asked him, saying, Master, who did sin, this man,
  or his parents, that he was born blind? Jesus answered, Neither hath
  this man sinned, nor his parents: but that the works of God should
  be made manifest in him (John 9:1–3).

- Trials reveal the glory of God:

  Now a certain man was sick, named Lazarus, of Bethany, the town
  of Mary and her sister Martha . . . therefore his sisters sent unto him,
  saying, Lord, behold, he whom thou lovest is sick. When Jesus heard
  that, he said, This sickness is not unto death, but for the glory of God,
  that the Son of God might be glorified thereby (John 11:1–4).

  Wherein ye greatly rejoice, though now for a season, if need be, ye
  are in heaviness through manifold temptations: that the trial of your
  faith, being much more precious than of gold that perisheth, though

it be tried with fire, might be found unto praise and honour and glory at the appearing of Jesus Christ (1 Peter 1:6–7).

- Trials reveal the love of God:

  For whom the Lord loveth he chasteneth, and scourgeth every son whom he receiveth (Hebrews 12:6).

- Trials reveal the favor of God:

  If ye endure chastening, God dealeth with you as with sons; for what son is he whom the father chasteneth not? But if ye be without chastisement, whereof all are partakers, then are ye bastards, and not sons (Hebrews 12:7–8).

- Trials reveal the comforting of God:

  Blessed be God, even the Father of our Lord Jesus Christ, the Father of mercies, and the God of all comfort; Who comforteth us in all our tribulation, that we may be able to comfort them which are in any trouble, by the comfort wherewith we ourselves are comforted of God (2 Corinthians 1:3–4).

- Trials reveal the compassion of God:

  Behold, we count them happy which endure. Ye have heard of the patience of Job, and have seen the end of the Lord; that the Lord is very pitiful, and of tender mercy (James 5:11).

Second, we suffer trials for the purpose of dealing with sin.

- Trials mete out consequences for sin:

  And the anger of the LORD was kindled against them; and he departed. And the cloud departed from off the tabernacle; and, behold, Miriam became leprous, white as snow: and Aaron looked upon Miriam, and, behold, she was leprous (Numbers 12:9–10).

And David said unto Nathan, I have sinned against the LORD. And Nathan said unto David, The LORD also hath put away thy sin; thou shalt not die. Howbeit, because by this deed thou hast given great occasion to the enemies of the LORD to blaspheme, the child also that is born unto thee shall surely die (2 Samuel 12:13–14).

- Trials bring us to repentance:

  And the LORD spake to Manasseh, and to his people: but they would not hearken. Wherefore the LORD brought upon them the captains of the host of the king of Assyria, which took Manasseh among the thorns, and bound him with fetters, and carried him to Babylon. And when he was in affliction, he besought the LORD his God, and humbled himself greatly before the God of his fathers, and prayed unto him: and he was intreated of him, and heard his supplication, and brought him again to Jerusalem into his kingdom. Then Manasseh knew that the LORD he was God (2 Chronicles 33:10–13).

Third, we suffer trials for the purpose of receiving instruction.

- Trials teach us God's Word:

  It is good for me that I have been afflicted; that I might learn thy statutes (Psalm 119:71).

- Trials teach us the importance of God's Word:

  And he humbled thee, and suffered thee to hunger, and fed thee with manna, which thou knewest not, neither did thy fathers know; that he might make thee know that man doth not live by bread only, but by every word that proceedeth out of the mouth of the LORD doth man live (Deuteronomy 8:3).

- Trials teach us faith:

And he said unto me, My grace is sufficient for thee: for my strength is made perfect in weakness. Most gladly therefore will I rather glory in my infirmities, that the power of Christ may rest upon me. Therefore I take pleasure in infirmities, in reproaches, in necessities, in persecutions, in distresses for Christ's sake: for when I am weak, then am I strong (2 Corinthians 12:9–10).

- Trials teach us contentment:

  Not that I speak in respect of want: for I have learned, in whatsoever state I am, therewith to be content. I know both how to be abased, and I know how to abound: every where and in all things I am instructed both to be full and to be hungry, both to abound and to suffer need (Philippians 4:11–12).

- Trials teach us humility:

  And lest I should be exalted above measure through the abundance of the revelations, there was given to me a thorn in the flesh, the messenger of Satan to buffet me, lest I should be exalted above measure (2 Corinthians 12:7).

- Trials teach us obedience:

  Though he were a Son, yet learned he obedience by the things which he suffered (Hebrews 5:8).

- Trials teach us endurance:

  And not only so, but we glory in tribulations also: knowing that tribulation worketh patience; and patience, experience; and experience, hope: and hope maketh not ashamed; because the love of God is shed abroad in our hearts by the Holy Ghost which is given unto us (Romans 5:3–4).

> *My brethren, count it all joy when ye fall into divers temptations; knowing this, that the trying of your faith worketh patience. But let patience have her perfect work, that ye may be perfect and entire, wanting nothing* (James 1:2–4).

- Trials teach us how to live righteously:

> *Now no chastening for the present seemeth to be joyous, but grievous: nevertheless afterward it yieldeth the peaceable fruit of righteousness unto them which are exercised thereby* (Hebrews 12:11).

- Trials teach us how to comfort others:

> *And whether we be afflicted, it is for your consolation and salvation, which is effectual in the enduring of the same sufferings which we also suffer: or whether we be comforted, it is for your consolation and salva-tion* (2 Corinthians 1:6).

Fourth, we suffer trials for other unique reasons.

- Trials bring others to Christ:

> *But I would ye should understand, brethren, that the things which happened unto me have fallen out rather unto the furtherance of the gospel; so that my bonds in Christ are manifest in all the palace, and in all other places; and many of the brethren in the Lord, waxing confident by my bonds, are much more bold to speak the word without fear* (Philippians 1:12–14).

> *Therefore I endure all things for the elect's sakes, that they may also obtain the salvation which is in Christ Jesus with eternal glory* (2 Timothy 2:10).

- Trials test our love for God:

> *Thou shalt not hearken unto the words of that prophet, or that*

dreamer of dreams: for the LORD your God proveth you, to know whether ye love the LORD your God with all your heart and with all your soul (Deuteronomy 13:3).

- Trials give us assurance of our own salvation:

  If ye endure chastening, God dealeth with you as with sons; for what son is he whom the father chasteneth not? But if ye be without chastisement, whereof all are partakers, then are ye bastards, and not sons (Hebrews 12:7–8).

- Trials refine and purify us:

  Wherein ye greatly rejoice, though now for a season, if need be, ye are in heaviness through manifold temptations: that the trial of your faith, being much more precious than of gold that perisheth, though it be tried with fire, might be found unto praise and honour and glory at the appearing of Jesus Christ (1 Peter 1:6–7).

- Trials prepare us for eternity:

  Yea doubtless, and I count all things but loss for the excellency of the knowledge of Christ Jesus my Lord: for whom I have suffered the loss of all things, and do count them but dung, that I may win Christ, and be found in him, not having mine own righteousness, which is of the law, but that which is through the faith of Christ, the righteousness which is of God by faith: that I may know him, and the power of his resurrection, and the fellowship of his sufferings, being made conformable unto his death (Philippians 3:8–10).

Appendix C

Practical Suggestions for Dealing with Illness

1. Keep seeking medical attention, taking prescribed medicines, and following doctor's guidelines.

2. Stay informed about your illness and possible treatments.

3. Learn your nutritional needs and follow healthful dietary principles.

4. Exercise as you are able to; be consistent even in small amounts.

5. Realize you have new limitations on your body and mind; seek to develop a routine according to this new normal.

6. Surround yourself with reminders of God's goodness and beauty—fresh flowers, good music, favorite colors, etc.

7. Build a support system of friends and family who can encourage and pray for you. Consider finding a support group of others in similar situations; make sure glorifying God is the focus of any such group.

8. Reach out to your friends when *you* feel discouraged or helpless.

9. Reach out to your friends when *they* feel discouraged or helpless.

10. Stop focusing on what you used to do and learn what you can do

now. Remember, you were wonderfully fashioned by the Creator, and no physical affliction can negate this truth.

11. Find new hobbies or activities you can enjoy in your present condition.

12. Look for ways to minister where you are right now.

13. Maintain an active prayer life; even the most disabled person can have a fruitful ministry of intercession.

14. Let others know specifically how to pray for you, and let them help bear your burdens before God.

15. Stay in God's Word. Read or listen to it daily. If possible, find an accountability partner to help you stay consistent in this practice.

16. Post Scripture verses around the house to see and meditate on regularly. Use this method to help memorize Scripture as well; it can be a great comfort when you are too sick to read God's Word.

17. Read plenty of Scripturally-centered theology and devotional books. Also, check out the mini-books at http://stores.newgrowthpress.com for resources on chronic pain, fatigue, and other medical problems.

18. Listen to godly preaching at church or online; there are plenty of free web site broadcasts available.

19. Keep a journal of God's provisions and blessings. Read through it whenever you need a reminder of God's faithfulness, love, and mercy.

20. Do not be too afraid or proud to ask for help.

Appendix D

Suggested Readings by Topic

CHARACTER OF GOD

Charnock, Stephen. *The Existence and Attributes of God: Volumes 1–2.* Ann Arbor, Michigan: Baker Book House Company, 1979.

This is an excellent resource on the person and character of God. Charnock covers a wide range of topics related to the study of God, including practical atheism, spiritual worship, the existence of God, and divine attributes. His studies in this area are considered to be some of the most in-depth resources available.

Pink, Arthur. *The Attributes of God.* Ann Arbor, Michigan: Bible Truth Depot, 1961.

This study on the perfection of God's character includes seventeen short chapters about various attributes, each with some bit of application to our personal lives.

Tozer, A.W. *The Attributes of God.* Camp Hill, Pennsylvania: Christian Publications, 1997.

A very readable, devotional-type of study, this book covers ten aspects of God's character. This is a classic work that includes plenty of Scripture, definitions, and personal application for each attribute. Tozer also asks a good number of reflective questions throughout the book, making it an excellent study for personal spiritual growth.

ATONEMENT OF CHRIST

Berkhof, Louis. *Vicarious Atonement through Christ.* Grand Rapids: Wm. B. Eerdmans Publishing Company, 1936.

Berkhof's work presents the centrality of the atonement to Christianity with its corresponding doctrine. He provides quite a few views, both accurate and inaccurate, and plenty of supporting research for each. This is a must-read for any in-depth study of the vicarious atonement of Christ.

Beilby, James and Eddy, Paul R., ed. *The Nature of the Atonement.* Downers Grove, IL: InterVarsity Press, 2006.

This book presents four major views of the atonement—Christus Victor, penal substitution, healing, and kaleidoscopic—and provides a response to each individual belief from the other three.

Murray, Andrew. *The Power of the Blood of Jesus.* Springdale, PA: Whitaker House, 1993.

A collection of lectures by Andrew Murray, this book focuses on the power of Christ's atonement as it applies to our daily lives. It begins with a biblical explanation of the atonement; it continues with the cleansing of, dwelling in, and finding victory through the blood of Christ.

Ryrie, Charles C. "Section X: So Great a Salvation." *Basic Theology.* Chicago: Moody Press, 1999.

This is a straightforward, down-to-earth explanation of the atonement, including its need and nature. Consider this an essential read for any believer of any maturity level.

GLORIFICATION OF BELIEVERS

Erickson, Millard J. "Part Ten: Salvation." *Introducing Christian Doctrine*. Grand Rapids: Baker Academic, 2001.

This is one of the few doctrinal study books covering the subject of glorification. In the section on salvation, Erickson includes the chapter, "The Continuation and Completion of Salvation," which includes sanctification, perseverance, and glorification. It gives a good overview of the doctrine of glorification, providing biblical support for confirmation and description of said promise.

PURPOSES OF SUFFERING

Schaeffer, Edith. *Affliction*. Old Tappan, New Jersey: Fleming H. Revell Company, 1978.

The title of this book speaks for itself: it looks in-depth at various reasons for and responses to affliction within a believer's life. Schaeffer herself was no stranger to suffering, and her sweet maturity from those trials comes through clearly in her words of hope and counsel.

Talbert, Layton. "Problems of Providence." *Not By Chance: Learning to Trust a Sovereign God*. Greenville, SC: Bob Jones University Press, 2001.

This chapter explores the question of sin being the cause of suffering; it also looks closely at whether Satan or God was the source of Job's suffering.

JAMES 5:14-16

Davids, Peter H. *The Epistle of James: A Commentary on the Greek Text*. Grand Rapids: Wm. B. Eerdmans Publishing Company, 1982.

This is a commentary written especially for those with knowledge of ancient Greek, as Davids writes out many of the original Greek words in their own language, supplementing similar and/or identical words from cross-references within the New Testament. Although the average reader could obtain greater understanding of the Scriptures from this work, it is better suited to the scholar who can fully grasp the uses and variants used within the original Greek manuscript.

Hiebert, D. Edmond. "Faith Tested by Its Resort to Prayer (5:13-18)." *The Epistle of James: Tests of a Living Faith*. Chicago: The Moody Bible Institute, 1979.

In this commentary on James, Hiebert provides an excellent exegetical look at each phrase of each verse within the entire epistle. Specifically, he denotes almost ten pages to verses 14–16, a passage which relates directly to the question of physical healing. Not only does Hiebert offer explanation of each phrase, but he includes definitions from the original Greek vocabulary used in James' epistle, providing a readable, yet in-depth look at this crucial passage of Scripture.

Robertson, A. T. "God and Medicine." *Studies in the Epistles of James*, 188–196. Nashville: Broadman Press, n.d.

Robertson's study of James reads more like a sermon than a commentary, which makes it well-suited for those with less academic training in the Scriptures (though all might profit from its reading). This particular section is weighted more toward application than exact interpretation, as he does not delve very deeply into some of the interpretational challenges surrounding this passage.

Tasker, R. V. G. *The General Epistle of James: An Introduction and Commentary*. Grand Rapids: Wm. B. Eerdmans Publishing Company, 1983.

Tasker provides a detailed exposition of each verse, often phrase-by-phrase. He includes cross-references, applicable quotes from church fathers (i.e., John Calvin), and a refutation of Roman Catholic practices, which were and are still prevalent today. It is very readable, not too simply written, but well-worded so even the average layperson can find a better understanding of the Word of God.

PRAYER

Bounds, E.M. *E.M. Bounds on Prayer.* New Kensington, PA: Whitaker House, 1997.

This comprehensive work is indeed a "rich inheritance of biblical research into the life of prayer," as the back cover of the book states. Bounds draws upon his own personal experience as well as in-depth biblical research as he pens chapter after chapter regarding the purpose, practice, and possibilities of prayer. Each chapter, though fairly short, contains quotations from church fathers or old hymns of the faith, illustrations from missionaries or other well-known believers, and a plethora of Scripture passages and principles. This is a powerful series for any believer who wants deeper and more effective communion with God.

Murray, Andrew. *Lord, Teach Us to Pray.* Philadelphia: Amazon Digital Services, 2011. Kindle file.

A short, powerful classic on the topic of prayer, this book looks closely at John 4:23–24 and Matthew 6:6–13. It is easy to follow and quite thought-provoking with its definitions, instruction, and applications to everyday life.

Ryle, J.C. *A Call to Prayer.* Laurel: Audubon Press, 2002.

This 33-page booklet contains seven piercing questions regarding prayer in the life of a believer, injunctions to those who do not pray or do not know God personally, and attributes that ought to characterize the believer's prayer life.

FAITH HEALING

Horton, Michael, ed. "Faith-Healing and the Sovereignty of God." *The Agony of Deceit.* Chicago: Moody Press, 1992.

This compilation of works by well-known Christian men includes Scripturally-based arguments against the heresy being proclaimed so prominently today, specifically via television. The noted chapter on faith healing is composed by C. Everett Koop, M.D., and provides a biblical and medical overview of this prominent controversy.

Macarthur, Jr., John F. *The Charismatics: A Doctrinal Perspective.* Grand Rapids: Zondervan Publishing House, 1979.

Two chapters in this comprehensive work cover "The Issue of Healing," and provide a clear case against modern so-called faith healers, contrasting their claims of miracles against the true gifts of healing shown by Christ and the apostles. Although this was written over thirty years ago, it is still quite applicable to today's world: some newer names may be available, but the principles are based in the timeless Word of God.

Warfield, Benjamin B. *Counterfeit Miracles.* Carlisle, Pennsylvania: The Banner of Truth Trust, 1995.

This classic work contains a series of lectures on the false doctrines of charismatics, the Roman Catholic Church, faith healers, and other cult practices. While the language and style is a bit difficult, its extensive studies cover myriad deceptions and false teachings, and it is incomparable in its field. The last two sections refer specifically to the topic of healing, but the entire book is well worth reading.

OTHER RESOURCES: HERMENEUTICS

Custer, Stewart. "Part II: The Use of Tools." *Tools for Teaching and Preaching the Bible.* Greenville, South Carolina: Bob Jones University Press, 1998.

McQuilken, Robertson. *Understanding and Applying the Bible.* Revised Edition. Chicago: Moody Press, 1992.

OTHER RESOURCES: BIBLE DICTIONARIES

"Heal, Healing." *Evangelical Dictionary of Theology.* 2nd Edition. Grand Rapids: Baker Academic, 2001.

"Healing." *New Dictionary of Biblical Theology.* Downers Grove, Illinois: InterVarsity Press, 2000.

"Health, Disease, and Healing." *New Bible Dictionary.* 3rd Edition. Downers Grove, Illinois: InterVarsity Press, 2004.

For more information about
Elizabeth A. Johnson
&
TOUCHING THE HEM
please visit:

Website: TouchingTheHemBook.com
Email: ejohnson@touchingthehembook.com
Twitter: @DogFurDandelion
Facebook: www.facebook.com/TouchingTheHem

For more information about
AMBASSADOR INTERNATIONAL
please visit:

www.ambassador-international.com
@AmbassadorIntl
www.facebook.com/AmbassadorIntl